THROUGH GRIEF-COLORED GLASSES

A Life Reinvented by Devastating Loss

VICKY EDGERLY

ANGEL DOG
PRODUCTIONS
NEW YORK

THROUGH GRIEF-COLORED GLASSES

A Life Reinvented by Devastating Loss

Copyright © 2025 by Vicky Edgerly

Published by:
Angel Dog Productions
244 Fifth Ave Suite N204
New York, NY 10001
(808) 280-5559
www.AngelDogProductions.com

Vicky Edgerly
www.WhiteElephantWisdom.com
vickyafterlife@gmail.com
+1 (603) 312-0091

ISBN: 979-8-9993383-0-3 (hard cover)
         979-8-9993383-1-0 (soft cover)
Library of Congress Control Number: 2025941978

Editor: Superior Book Productions
Cover Design/Interior Book Layout: Nicole Gabriel, Let's Get Your Book Published

Every attempt has been made to properly source all quotes.
In some instances, names have been changed to protect individuals' privacy.

Printed in the United States of America
First Edition

2 4 6 8 10 12

DEDICATION

For my three:

Adam, Tierra, and Leo, who through death taught me how to live.

Until we meet again…xo

ACKNOWLEDGMENTS

As you can imagine, getting a story like mine down on paper in a meaningful way was a daunting task for someone who has never written a book before. It took me twenty years to bring this memoir into the world, and the list of folks, both here on earth and beyond, who helped me along the way is quite immense. From my friend Donna, who showed me the importance of having someone unafraid to bear witness to my pain by standing wordlessly next to me at my son's grave when we buried him, to my good friend Cheryl, who didn't say, "It's about time!" when she learned my book was ready to publish, but instead congratulated me on a job well done, I have been supported by lovely people.

While the grief journeys were solo endeavors, something I had to travel predominantly alone, a supporting cast of characters within my story often unknowingly helped egg me on along my way by dropping a golden nugget of information in a seemingly innocent conversation or by providing living examples of theories and beliefs I could then employ to prompt another layer of my own healing and use as fodder to show others the way through their own.

My sister Linda has been constant throughout my story, and as you'll learn in the coming pages, was closely involved with all three deaths and resulting grief journeys. She discovered my son's lifeless body, was instrumental in helping me care for my dying daughter, and was the first on the scene the day my husband shot himself. Her steadfast presence has served as an anchor to help keep me grounded in the reality I experienced.

My volunteer work with The Afterlife Education Foundation, founded by Rev. Dr. Terri Daniel, and its annual conferences gave me my first look into what it would be like to bring a story like mine into an open, public forum. The positive feedback I received from colleagues and bereaved attendees certainly validated my work and illustrated our society's hunger for a deeper understanding of death and the grief journey. It encouraged me to move forward with my own project whenever I felt insecure or doubted its worth in the world.

I would be remiss if I didn't mention my writing coach and book designer, Nicole Gabriel, from Let's Get Your Book Published. Without her help, I never would have gotten this book over the finish line. Her immense knowledge of the publishing world and easy manner of supporting and directing my efforts while still honoring my own personal process and the sacredness of this project places her at the head of the pack in my book (pun intended), and a simple "Thank you" seems inadequate. Her expertise was truly invaluable.

Nicole also introduced me to Tyler Tichelaar from Superior Book Productions who brought his professional editing skills to the table. With his help, we added the polish my writing needed, transforming a good story into a fantastic book. Tyler's supportive feedback and encouragement guided my hand in placing the finishing touches, and I am grateful to have had him in my corner during this last step before sharing this book with the world.

And finally, my heartfelt thanks go out to all the grieving people who have trusted me with their pain in group and/or private sessions and those I encounter throughout my daily life whose stories of loss come out in unexpected, synchronistic meetings of the mind and heart. Hearing I have helped dispel some of the fear in their grief and watching them blossom into healthier, happier people allows me to truly see and understand the great value in this work that has chosen me in this lifetime. For this, I am eternally grateful.

CONTENTS

INTRODUCTION

I've known since my eighteen-year-old son Adam took his own life on Mother's Day back in 2002 that I would one day write a book about my experience. I imagined my words would help people. Help them feel they were not alone in their suffering and help inspire them to face each day knowing others have walked the same path before them and survived.

I'd fill the book with harrowing stories of how the unimaginable had happened to me, and yet here I am, still standing and functioning in a world where children die by their own hand. I'd weave the tale of what a beautiful boy my son had been so readers like you would love him as much as I do. And if you loved him, you would not judge him for taking his own life and leaving the rest of us who adored him in shattered pieces. But the words would not flow.

A mere eight years later, the unimaginable happened—again. The big "C" visited our family and took my daughter Tierra with it when it left not long after her thirtieth birthday. *Aha!* I thought. *Perhaps I hadn't been able to finish my book because God, the Universe, or my own Soul somehow knew what was to come, and this book needed to be about losing both of my kids.* Who could possibly read such a story and not be uplifted by hope?

Still, the book would not write itself. Why? Caring for my daughter during her long illness certainly took its toll on me, so perhaps I just needed some time to heal. Once again, I put the project down and took the pressure of an imagined deadline off my plate. The grieving masses I was to help would just have to wait.

> *"I cannot lead the way for you while I am still blind."*
> *(Excerpt from the song, "Home" by Vicky Edgerly)*

As if the loss of my two children wasn't enough, two years after my daughter's death, my second husband, Leo, shot himself dead on our beautiful property, and grief brought me to my knees once more. In the days following his suicide, I realized I still had that familiar *knowing* I would, indeed, write this book. But my perception of it began to change…along with my entire life, effectively setting me up for how the writing would unfold when the timing was finally right. However, all this loss wasn't only about writing a book.

Of course, I have my own reason for wanting to publish my story as a sort of legacy for my descendants. It's a way for my grandchildren (and the generations that spring from them) to know who their mother was as a young woman suffering from a terminal illness, knowing she'd have to leave her three young children behind, and a chance to learn more about their uncle Adam, who died when the eldest of them was only two, the other two not yet born.

In addition, they would be able to revisit a very pivotal time in their young lives, armed with the gift of their own maturity and a fair bit of hindsight. There they could take a closer look at all the players in the drama they participated in so long ago as little kids with varying abilities to understand what was happening around them.

But why would I want to share such an intimate look inside my private life with you and the world at large? The simplest and most straightforward answer is I'm writing the book I wish I had access to after my son's death in 2002, and I want it to be available to those who come after me while facing similar pain and heartache. I saw a great need, and I decided someone had to fill it, so it might as well be me.

When faced with the devastation following Adam's suicide, I quickly discovered I was ill-prepared to process that kind of all-encompassing pain and anguish, and no programs or support groups in my community offered any tangible path to genuine healing.

Since American culture tends to shield and protect children from dark subjects such as death and grief, I had no education whatsoever growing up that would help me handle such an event. When my son died, I was essentially left to my own devices, feeling lost as I struggled to find a way through with a lasting impression from my childhood that death was only to be whispered about behind closed doors and something we should all fear.

I didn't have much of a religious background growing up, so I did not have a familiar church family or clergy member to turn to, no practiced relationship with God, or clear understanding of heaven beyond the common belief that *I'll get to see him again once I join him in heaven*, which essentially translates to: *I'd have to die myself before I'd be able to reach my lost boy.*

Since I had no practice of faith to lean on and my local grief support group failed to offer anything beyond a "misery loves company" fellowship, I turned to books and internet research. I found lots of technical data and even some stories written from the author's experience. But while I did encounter little nuggets of hope and insight in some of those texts, none offered a comprehensive way to approach the task of healing.

Because my trauma-shocked brain was not operating at full capacity, it was beyond my scope at the time to pull any real action steps from the information I was reading. I needed a strategy, something that showed me which steps to take to move me forward on this path I learned to call "The Grief Journey." Since I could not find an existing plan to guide me, I did the only thing I could think of at the time. I simply decided I would survive, feeling my way forward through the dark by instinct alone. I would have to blaze the trail myself.

That was the first and, as it turns out, most important step. I didn't know it at the time, but I was at a crossroads of sorts, and my decision to move forward and seek deeper healing than society offered at the time paved the way for the work I am doing now, assisting others like you through life's most painful events.

As I explored that rough and arduous terrain, a world where my beloved son would never grow past the tender age of eighteen, I unearthed treasures beyond measure. Because during that virgin dance with grief and loss I found my faith and spirituality, which became my lifeline during the difficult years yet to come.

Among all the books, articles, and even medical and psychological journals I read, nothing sparked hope (and eventually excitement!) like my forays into the world of spirituality, metaphysics, and energy work. Keeping an open mind, I dove into whatever made me "feel better," and I soon realized the teachings, meditation, and energy healing sessions were bringing me gifts I never even knew existed.

These healing tools brought me peace of mind and calmed my anxieties like no friends or family ever could. They helped me discover things about myself and how my psyche worked. They helped me foster a greater understanding of the nature of the Soul and what we are truly capable of creating and experiencing. They taught me I actually have a choice in any given situation of how I will experience (and react to) what is happening based simply on what I taught my brain to believe, freeing me from the misplaced belief that I would never recover from such a loss. And best of all, these methods and concepts taught me how to establish a relationship with my son while in his newfound state of disembodied soul, something I didn't even know was possible!

Choosing to find my own way through debilitating grief has led me not only to write the book you're holding in your hands, but to usher into the world an innovative and effective grief support system, called "Dragonfly Wisdom: A Holistic Approach to Grief Support," that can be easily implemented by groups large or small anywhere in the world. Simply put, I have developed the step-by-step grief support program I needed when I felt so lost and broken after Adam left this world in such a violent way.

By organizing more than two decades' worth of intense personal experience, observation, and research into one easy-to-follow manual, I am finally able to share my work with larger groups and communities, effectively helping more people. It is my heart's desire to bring hope to those who believe the light has gone out of their lives forever after experiencing a significant, debilitating loss. I simply can't finish my life here on earth without leaving a beacon for those still trying to find their way out of the dark.

After hearing my story, if you are like most people I have encountered throughout the years, you may be thinking, *How on earth did she survive such loss? How is she still standing and functioning?* or *How does she even get up each morning?*

Historically, when met with such questions, I would be at a loss to explain my process of becoming the emotionally and spiritually sound being who stood before them. I didn't know how to articulate it beyond the phrase, "I chose to survive." I couldn't sum it up in conversation, email, or blog posts. I realized it was much too big to simply tell people about; instead, I'd somehow have to find a way to *show* them—and you.

"Those who learned to know death, rather than to fear and fight it, become our teachers about life."

— Elisabeth Kubler-Ross

LET THE DEAD LEAD THE WAY

At the time of this writing, I am sixty years old, and I have reached a point where I can look back on my story with the kind of fondness one feels for a comfortable old car that has been with them for years with all its dings and dents, safely transporting them to destinations filled with fun and exciting adventures. And like all good adventures, my story is riddled with danger and hardships that usher in powerful opportunities for the heroine to rise to the challenge, overcome, and triumph all the while growing stronger, wiser, and more capable of leading others through similar adversities.

When I think of all the places my story has taken me, I conjure up the various passengers who rode with me for the most poignant chapters, especially those who are considered lost to this world, those who took the wheel during the parts of my story they each commanded in turn through their respective deaths. Then I thought, *Why not let them take the wheel again now for the telling of it? Why not let each of them play the leading role in their own drama?* But how would I give them each a voice that others could hear? The answer was right in front of me in the form of an overstuffed file folder in a desk drawer.

The folder was filled with tangible, savable mementos from each of my three lost loved ones—photos, greeting cards, and poems written by my daughter, Tierra; drawings, handwritten notes scrawled on kitchen notepads, and funeral cards I kept after my son Adam died; and news articles, old driver's licenses, and love letters saved from my time with my husband Leo—all stored away in that drawer.

As I sifted through those old treasures, I could see Leo and my kids clearly in my mind's eye, as they were in life, each with their own unique and individual personality. I could hear their voices, remember their smiles, and hear their signature laughs.

But I also saw something else. I saw the progression of my own healing journey in the various letters, notes, and song lyrics I wrote to each of them along the way. It was all there in that drawer—evidence of the broken, lost, confused woman I was after Adam hanged himself on Mother's Day in 2002. A letter I wrote to him after waking from a particularly disturbing dream I didn't understand was placed alongside notes written months or years later thanking him for his frequent "dream visits" that I eventually learned to treasure.

I could see the frantic, almost "bargaining with God" attitude I had in my early writings to my daughter during her long illness. In saved greeting cards, I continued to push my agenda of helping her beat the cancer that came to claim her life. Nestled right next to those cards was a piece I wrote about what it felt like to finally surrender to what was happening and turn my attention and efforts to helping her die instead of trying to force her to live.

And finally, I recognized the incredible strength and quiet power I embodied shining through in the beautiful eulogy I wrote and delivered at the celebration of life event I hosted on our property after Leo left this world, leaving me humbled by all that had happened and so very grateful to all three of them for the help and guidance they had provided along the way.

It seemed to me that a formal letter of thanks was long overdue, and so I began to pour out my feelings and memories in new letters to each of them in turn, realizing it was the perfect way to bring my story to life in a "lead by example" kind of way. I had found a way to show you, the reader, after all. A way in which each of their personalities could break through my narrative so they could be heard and seen in a way that brings you into the story itself as a quiet observer to these private and revealing conversations.

The following is an intimate account of what it was like for me to walk through each of these significant losses and the resulting grief journeys, each one clearly as unique as the person who died, yet woven together with similar challenges anyone acquainted with acute grief will recognize. And because all grief is different, being unique due to the different relationships we have with the deceased along with varying circumstances surrounding their deaths, I can show you how I not only survived the pain and loss, but I actually used it to grow…and eventually, offer my hard-earned wisdom as a gift to the world for others, like you, to benefit from.

You'll have a front row seat as I explain to my husband and children what it was like for me to live so many years of my life in a world without them, and you'll benefit from the additional bits of wisdom I gained by dissecting my journey now that I'm in my sixties and looking back at it all.

If you have suffered a painful loss, you will undoubtedly see yourself within these pages. It is my hope you will come away with a deeper sense of peace and know you, too, can enjoy a fulfilling life even while experiencing grief. And if you haven't lost anyone close to you but expect to one day, your curiosity has also brought you to the right place because you will gain insights within these pages that will help shape your perceptions of death and grief, making your future journeys through the pain of loss less intimidating.

Regardless of your motives for picking up this book, you are welcome here. I invite you in for an intimate conversation about life's most difficult things. I invite you in to bear witness to my story, and I thank you for sticking with me through it. I invite you to feel what I felt, the good, the bad, and the ugly, and I invite you to be lifted and inspired by my moments of accomplishment and joyful self-realization along the way.

So, settle in for the ride as we look at what it's like to rebuild one's life while viewing the world *through grief-colored glasses*.

"We bereaved are not alone. We belong to the largest company in all the world—the company of those who have known suffering."

— Clover Stroud

PART ONE

ADAM

CHAPTER 1

DON'T BELIEVE EVERYTHING THEY SAY

They say that what doesn't kill us makes us stronger. They also say there is no coming back after losing a child. Statements like these are prevalent in our society, made evident by our ability to recall and recite them word for word whenever fitting circumstances arise. We innocently parrot back such sentiments to each other without really taking a moment to think about where the statement originated and whether it is actually true. We certainly never consider the lasting imprint that hearing such statements might leave on the recipient, especially if they are in a vulnerable state.

By now, you know I have lost not one but both of my children, and yet here I am, still standing and enjoying a life full of rich experiences with a childlike sense of curiosity and wonder when faced with the unknown of what my future may bring. I think it's safe to say I am living proof that the *no coming back from losing a child* statement is undeniably a lie, for I most definitely have come back.

As you move through the ten-year timeline of my story, taking note of the confused and somewhat broken woman I was after the shock of my son's suicide, you will clearly see the strength and wisdom I gained as I felt my way instinctively through a self-healing process during successive significant losses, proving the first statement quite true. My experiences definitely did not kill me but, indeed, made me stronger.

The journey was treacherous to be sure, and at times, I felt I was being led through the lowest points by unseen forces since I had no idea where to start, but I always somehow stumbled upon just the right concept, theory, practice, or modality when I needed it most.

A perfect example is when I, the forty-year-old woman ravaged by the shocking news of her eighteen-year-old son's death by suicide, made a conscious decision to simply survive that atrocity, for I could have just as easily believed I would never recover from an *unnatural* loss such as the death of a child. I could have taken that on as my truth and sank into the depths of despair, closing my heart off never to smile, laugh, or love again. Then I realized I actually had a choice.

I find a kind of poetic justice steeped in irony that my son, Adam, first brought my attention to these old sayings, quotes, and wives' tales. He relentlessly chastised me for falling back on them at every turn during our mother/son relationship, calling upon them to teach him things like "Money doesn't grow on trees," or "When life feels hard, just go with the flow."

My memory of this aspect of our life together prompted me to take a closer look at what I consciously told my brain to believe versus old beliefs I had running in the background on autopilot. That curiosity to explore my ability to choose my own thoughts and beliefs would form one of the cornerstones of my grief support work.

Writing a letter to Adam at this stage of my life has not only brought a deeper level of healing and closure to me personally, but it has provided me with an overview of my entire recovery process along with clear steps forward for developing a program others can truly benefit from. I could plainly see it all taking shape within the following pages, starting with my newly formed answer when I would be asked, "How did you do it? How did you survive?" Today, I can sum it all up in the following three steps:

1. Decide to survive. (We *do* have a choice.)

2. Attend to one sore spot at a time. (Focus on where you are *now*, not looking back or ahead.)

3. Digging up bones. (Replace old and damaging beliefs with more empowering ones.)

I would be remiss to open the door to my conversation with Adam without first addressing the very large *elephant in the room* (another popular saying used to describe something on everyone's mind that no one has the courage to speak of out loud), and that is suicide.

Losing a loved one by suicide is a particularly challenging event to recover from, especially when that loved one was your own child. We are taught that it's a parent's job to protect their children at all costs, so what kind of mother was I to let my own child end their life in that way? What did I fail to do that would have made him stay? Or was there something I did do that caused his discomfort and sent him into depression? Something in the way I raised him? Something in the DNA I passed on to him?

Those kinds of thoughts, left unchecked, would have embedded themselves deeply into my psyche, eventually becoming part of my operating system going forward, forever shaping all future events and relationships I would encounter in my lifetime.

The attitudes of others in my community also posed a challenge for me while I made efforts to recover and heal. Folks commonly react with anger and disgust toward the perpetrator…the one who caused all the pain and anguish…the one who chose to *take the easy way out* and leave everyone else with the proverbial mess to clean up.

These accusatory sentiments often went unsaid when I was in earshot, but they were present in the form of a very large, palpable energy, a dark and looming unspoken thing, a.k.a. an elephant in the room with us. I could feel and sense these attitudes, and it angered me that, as a society, we still keep discussions around suicide closeted or whispered in secret instead of bringing them into open and authentic dialogues.

Had any one of them been brave enough to say those things to me, I would have invited a conversation about it, pointing out my perspective— one of a mother who had to realize and accept that her boy was in enough emotional pain to make the unknown state of death seem more desirable than living one more day in his current situation. Knowing that, how could I possibly respond with anger toward him for the discomfort he was causing *me* for having lost him in this way? When faced with that particular choice, I elected to respond with compassion and empathy toward my beautiful boy.

As we move through this book together, I will act as your guide, occasionally popping in to set the stage, offer a little backstory, or expand on a specific concept if required. But, at the end of the day, you are free to roam about the pages at will with my blessing. And when you close this book after reading the last page, may you leave behind all the pain and anguish you witnessed here and, instead, choose to take with you a newfound sense of peace and the curiosity to explore a broader understanding of your own life.

Dear Adam,

You were such an entertaining kid. We couldn't take our eyes off you when you were on one of your highs. You commanded the room with your smile, your animated chatter, and your uncanny wit for a child of your size. You had what we might call charisma. Yes, even as a boy of four years old, you had charisma...bucket loads.

Your life was one big drama. The ups were where you shined, of course, as the center of your own universe, drawing others in like moths to a flame. So beautiful, so funny, so charming.

But your lows were damaging, singeing the wings of the moths who ventured too close, unaware that the brightest of lights could flare up and burn at any moment, causing pain and often leaving scars.

You didn't seem aware of the effect you had on others, as if being the light prevented you from seeing the light. Perhaps the brightness of who you were was somehow incinerating you from the inside. Perhaps the burden of being so adored was too much for you to carry, my son. Perhaps.

You chose Mother's Day, and our home together, as the stage for your final exit scene. Would it surprise you to know that reassured me? Knowing you felt safe enough to carry out this most intimate act in the home I had made for the two of us allowed me to feel I was able to offer comfort to you in some small way during those last few moments of your life, and the Happy Mother's Day call before you left I, of course, will cherish forever.

You tried to tell me you were leaving. In your own way, you tried to say goodbye. Only in hindsight can I hear it in the "Mom? I love you" when our habit was more of a "Luv ya" kind of thing. That more formal declaration of love as you were hanging up the phone that day was your goodbye.

We found out later, after hearing stories from others, that you had spent the previous day and evening visiting old friends and your mood was serious, subdued, and humble. You were not your normal animated self. No sarcastic jibes were delivered and no witty jokes told with the uncanny precision of a well-seasoned professional comedian.

Instead, you brought up old stories with each friend of fond memories and good times spent with them over the years. You even apologized to some, making right the things you realized you had said or done that were less than kind. You were putting your affairs in order.

I hope all who received those parting gifts from you saw them as just that, a final gift, rather than allowing such memories to haunt them. After all, the "I should haves" or "If I had only knowns" or "Why didn't I see what was happening and stop him?" do not serve any purpose other than to trap us in the lower vibration of guilt and fear, a useless waste of our time and energy that often leads to prolonged grief and symptoms of depression. But I had yet to learn that for myself.

Ah the grief…that was an entity that, seemingly, could not be tamed.

Twenty years ago, I didn't know anything about our so-called vibration and how it affects our everyday experience. I had no clue I could shape my life by purposely training my thought patterns. I was also completely unaware that the methods I would eventually use to teach myself and others how to navigate traumatic loss would be considered "woo woo" or "New Age" and, therefore, shunned and even scorned by a large portion of our society.

Not until the day you left this world did I develop a passion (bordering on obsession) for the study of all things paranormal, mystical, or otherworldly. Mind you, I had no interest in learning about aliens or doing any ghost hunting, attending any séances, or contacting any famous characters from the past, no...I simply had a driving need to know where you went and if you were really at peace like people of certain faiths kept telling me you were.

I'm sure it's no surprise to you that I was shocked and "traumatized" by your suicide. In the midst of my daily efforts to just get through, I was also struggling with the opinion you simply ceased to exist once you had stopped your body's heart from beating and ended your earthly life.

"They'd have me believe, that you ceased to exist.
What loving God would cast me into such an abyss?"
(Excerpt from the song "Surviving the Storm" by Vicky Edgerly)

But if by some slim chance there actually was some kind of afterlife where you'd still be able to interact with me and be part of my life, why the hell wouldn't I put everything I had into learning all about that? Why wouldn't everyone do that when faced with the pain of this kind of loss? How could anyone in their right mind just "let go" and assume nothing further was to be done?

Faith, they said. I was told I had to have faith that I would one day get to see you again in heaven where you now enjoyed a peaceful rest—that I could trust this was the truth and take comfort in knowing all I had to do was wait until it was my time to go. But when have you ever known your mother to sit still and do nothing while waiting?

I needed answers, so I made it my mission to find them. I'll tell you one thing. You'd have been proud of your mom for not giving up! Like Hansel and Gretel's famous breadcrumb trail, I found clues along the way. Without any instructions, I was able to sense some pretty important things right at the start, the first one being that I in no way would accept any responsibility for your choice to leave when you did.

I somehow understood, quite clearly mind you, that it was something you decided for yourself and carried out all on your own, and it was not my job to bear the guilt that would surely drown me if I were to accept the blame for your suicide. My survival depended on it, and I instinctively knew it.

In the beginning, I had trouble saying the word "dead." I could not come right out and say you had died, could not speak words like, "Adam died," or "Adam is dead," or God forbid, "Adam committed suicide," "Adam killed himself," and most certainly not, "Adam hanged himself." What I could say was, "After what happened to Adam" or

"When Adam chose to leave" along with a handful of other awkward-sounding euphemisms that allowed me to avoid the words death and suicide.

I can't remember how much time went by before I started noticing I was stumbling over myself to circumvent those poisonous words, but as soon as I did, I began to force myself to do the uncomfortable thing. I had to say the words and phrases that made it all real…all final. I don't know how I knew, but I was certain it was imperative I face those things head-on during my journey.

I wondered if, by saying Adam died out loud, I had somehow moved into the phase of grief they call acceptance. I don't know if you ever came across it in your lifetime, but "they" (as in intellectuals, scholars, and mental health professionals) have pushed this sort of schedule of grieving on society for decades. They call it the five stages of grief and name them in this order: denial, anger, bargaining, depression, and acceptance.

So…did I skip to the end of class, my grief over because I had come to accept what you had done to yourself? Or was I simply moving out of the first stage of denial, which would mean I was moving into anger? But I didn't feel angry. Not at you. Well, maybe a little angry when I realized how badly the adventurous summer I had planned with my new love, Leo was going to suck because of all the heavy emotions I would have to lug around with me. Admittedly, I was a little angry about that. But not at you. I wasn't angry with you at all, just the situation I was in.

As much as it horrifies any new friends I meet to learn you hanged yourself a mere twenty minutes after wishing me a happy Mother's Day on the phone, I always understood it was not meant to be a statement or accusation, not a personal attack on me as your mother. I'm sure it wasn't your plan. I'm sure it simply happened to be the day you needed to do this thing. But Jesus, Adam, that caused a bit of a ruckus in the community!

I have lots of memories that have twisted, turned, and reshaped themselves into something different over the years and rearranged themselves on the earthly timeline, but the memory of receiving the news of your death has remained quite vivid in detail to this day. Were you watching this unfold from your new perspective, Adam?

Even though I had just been released the night before from a weeklong hospital stay, still suffering from the disorienting headaches that a bout with spinal meningitis had left me, I remember already "knowing" something was wrong long before the news came. I don't know if it was a mother's intuition or what, but I felt it was taking you too long to arrive for our planned visit. Something wasn't right.

When the knock came at the door, and I glanced up from my movie (I'll never forget I was watching *Fried Green Tomatoes* while you hanged yourself in our home just a few miles away), I saw Leo, who was doing dishes at the kitchen sink, reach over to let my sister in.

The whispering between them barely registered in my foggy, pain-filled brain because I was fixated on two things my mind could not quite reconcile: 1) Why was my sister here at my door when I had just talked to her on the phone a half hour ago, and she assured me nothing was amiss and you were fine, and 2) Who was the strange woman following her through the door into Leo's home?

I strained to focus so I could understand what was happening in the kitchen. Leo seemed to be acting very scattered and nervous. He was trying to keep the two women out of the living room where I was still seated, no…cemented really to an easy chair in front of the TV. He was insisting they let him put a shirt on first. This made absolutely no sense, and something deep inside me threw up protective barriers as I prepared myself for what would happen next.

Honestly, Adam, since you were supposed to be bringing your niece, little Skyla, with you for a Mother's Day visit because your sister was away for the weekend, I immediately assumed it would be a car wreck with something terrible happening to the child. I braced myself for the worst.

But still, my brain could not connect what it was prepared to hear with what was actually said. "Skyla is fine. She is at Tammy's house," Linda assured me. I hung my head, grateful my granddaughter was safely tucked away at my sister's childhood friend's home where she would be cared for like family, but resigned to receive the bad news that I could feel coming at me like a freight train.

"Where is Adam? What happened to him?" I asked.

"I'm sorry, Vicky. He's dead. He hanged himself." Linda announced.

Many believe God never gives us more than we can handle, and of course, what doesn't kill us makes us stronger. While your death eventually led me on a wonderful journey of self-discovery, where I purposely went looking for old and damaging beliefs within my psyche to be rooted out, these two I decided to keep. These two beliefs would set the stage for how my grief journey would play out. They very quickly became my truth, my mantras. I would become stronger from the experience. But it would be a very long time before I could claim that statement as my truth.

Since you were only eighteen when you left, you hadn't had the chance to start a family of your own, so you probably can't even imagine what it would feel like to be a mother receiving such news about her youngest child, her golden boy. Because that's what you were, Adam. You were my golden boy. Your shine was so bright that you lit up any room you entered. You captivated audiences of all genders and ages with your charm, intelligence, and wit, not to mention your "tall, dark, and handsome" good looks. I was so proud to be your mom.

I remember how brilliant you were. I know all mothers think their offspring is the prettiest, smartest, funniest, and all-around best kid ever, but Adam, you truly were! And it wasn't just me who thought it. Everyone did. I regularly received reports of your star-like qualities from family and friends. If only the "other side" of you wasn't so dark.

If I have any regrets at all, it's that I didn't recognize just how difficult it was for you to exist when your moods swung you down into the lower vibrational realms. I had no idea you struggled to actually stay on the planet with the rest of us, so I did very little to help you navigate, assuming you'd eventually outgrow what I believed was "normal" teenage sullenness and settle into making a nice life for yourself. How could I know what I didn't know?

My behavior toward your mood swings was learned early in your life. You taught me if I just exercised a little bit of patience, your attitude would naturally swing back up all on its own. It was then, when you were feeling lighter, I would find my openings to have meaningful conversations with you. Only in that brighter state of mind would you be able to remain open enough to receive my words and accept my guidance. So that was our pattern—yours and mine. You'd go off the rails, and I would sit tight, watching and waiting for my opportunity to reach you when the dust settled.

Well, I couldn't reach you that day, Adam. I was barely functioning myself with lingering pain and confusion from the meningitis, focusing all my cerebral efforts on just understanding the story being played out on the television that morning. I wouldn't have been able to offer much in my state. I didn't have the tools or the wherewithal to help you then.

Fried Green Tomatoes. It's funny how we can't know exactly how a situation or event will affect us until after the fact. We can't know which wounds will heal and which ones will leave permanent scars. While the whole world seemed to watch, expecting me to be forever traumatized by Mother's Day, it was actually the movie that took the hit.

The day you died was probably the third or fourth time I had watched that movie since its release in 1991. It was one of my favorites, and I loved rewatching it. Ask me what the story is about today, and I couldn't tell you. Zero, zilch, no memory whatsoever.

So, what does your mother do when she comes face to face with a realization such as the one above (because I really am just realizing the truth in that statement now, as I write it)? I just added *Fried Green Tomatoes* to my watchlist. I will watch that movie again soon—for the first time in twenty years, and release what I hope to be one of the final remaining layers of buried grief and trauma over your choice to die on Mother's Day so long ago.

That's my method. That's how I did it and continue to do it. That's how I survived, by rooting out and tending to one sore spot at a time. Obviously, I had to address the gaping hole in my heart first to stop hemorrhaging my very life's essence, but now, after all this time, I am somewhat surprised to find I still have more work to do.

It's ironic really, Adam, that all my efforts along the way to learn healthy ways to work through my grief have actually given me many tools and skills you could have used to help understand and navigate your own challenges when you were young.

I'd be lying if I said I didn't wish things could have been different. I'd be lying if I said I never went down the "what if" trail. I mean, who wouldn't? The trick, though, is to act once you notice you're doing it. And the action I'd take was making a conscious decision to turn away from that type of thinking and find ways to direct my thoughts in a healthier, more empowering way.

These practices became lifelines for me after you died. I only wish I could have acquired them all at once instead of being fed them piecemeal, one at a time, while following a sometimes very painful, decades-long quest to discover the secrets of the universe.

It would have made life a lot easier that's for sure, but really, would it have been better? I mean, quests and treasure hunts are pretty fun, right? After all, it's the journey, not the destination, that holds all the bounty. Isn't that what they say?

I can see you rolling your eyes. I remember how much it annoyed you when I used quotes, euphemisms, and old wives' tales to teach you about life during our conversations as mother and son. I didn't know it then, but later, after your death and my resulting journey of self-discovery, I would become obsessed with that old habit. Why? Because I discovered their value as tools to help train my brain to believe what I wanted it to, because that little revelation (that my brain will believe anything I tell it) was the "key to the kingdom." (Now you're outright laughing because it seems I can't even finish a paragraph without tossing an old saying into the mix.)

Alas, that's when the real roller-coaster ride began. The journey to root out old beliefs that play out in my subconscious without my awareness of what kind of havoc they were wreaking in the background was a slippery slope to be sure, but a labor of love (and necessity!) nonetheless, for I simply would not accept the common belief that "There is no coming back from something like this." I had to believe a full recovery from this painful experience we call *grief* was indeed possible, and I made it my personal mission to prove it could be done.

One of the first things I became aware of was, of course, the widespread belief, "It's unnatural for a child to die before their parents." But there I was with a child to bury. My brain couldn't come to terms with that statement, couldn't find any truth in it, yet today we have come to believe it.

I can't tell you how many people actually said those words to me after your death. I could never figure out how it was supposed to make me feel. I had survived the unimaginable, the worst atrocity life could dole out had been given to me, according to those in the know, and so I wondered, was I being asked to feel like the chosen one or something since this thing where children die first is such an unnatural event?

Then there's the strength everyone talks about. People were telling me how strong I was because my kid had died. Died by his own hand, on Mother's Day! "I could never survive that. You're so strong!" they'd say, fawning over me like some kind of celebrity. Again, I'm not sure if those comments were supposed to shore me up and make me feel larger than life, but what they actually did was put pressure on me to act strong around other people because they clearly expected it of me, and Lord knows, a people-pleaser like I was at the time would be more than happy to give the masses what they wanted. Sigh....

But somewhere deep within my sore brain, which was limping along with its circuits fried from the shock of your violent death (Who hangs themselves anyway? We'll need to unpack that one at some point, son…another day), I was able to push back against that one statement. "It's unnatural for a child to die before their parents."

Well, your method of death may not have been "natural," but other people lose children to disease, accidents, and even horrendous events like murder every day, so it is, indeed a "naturally occurring event." For us as a society to hold on to such an erroneous belief only sets us all up for unnecessary hardship in the future, should we ever have to experience such a loss ourselves. Why do we all bury our heads in the sand when it comes to the ever-present and commonly occurring subject of death?

I'm proud of me, you know, for now being able to say "dead," "dying," and "death" with ease. I can now say those words without flinching or being triggered in any way. They say once you are no longer triggered by the things that previously sent you diving for cover, you have healed. I don't know if it's possible to be completely healed from something like this, Adam. Much like some of the old injuries in my body, I feel like my wounds over losing you are now faded scars. And if the experience dampened my ability to fully relax, leaving me with a slight undercurrent of anxiety, well, then I will consider myself one of the lucky ones for I am still standing—still functioning and still enjoying my life.

Although my intellectual abilities were impaired by the shock of my son's suicide, leaving me unable to think and reason properly, it seems I was still somehow able to operate at "intuitive levels." Becoming hyper-focused on something that didn't quite make sense to me, like noticing how odd it made me feel when people said things like, "It's not fair! A child is not supposed to die before their parents," quickly became a pattern that developed into one of my greatest strengths.

Even though I wouldn't be in any shape to help others with their own pain for quite some time, it seemed I was already instinctively getting to the root of the matter as far as my own immediate needs went. Do you recall the three basic principles of effectively processing grief I mentioned at the beginning of this chapter? Here is how the list was going for me even in the early days after my first experience with significant loss.

1. **Decide to survive. (We *do* have a choice.)** Making a conscious decision not to accept any blame for my son's choice to die was a "survival choice," and I instinctively knew it at the time. That was my first opportunity to choose my own survival over victimhood. Chances to reinforce and strengthen my decision to count myself as a survivor would present themselves along the way, giving me the option to slip into victimhood at any time. But making that very first observation about my choice to refuse the blame offered my brain all the proof it needed that I did, indeed, have a choice in all of this.

2. **Attend to one sore spot at a time. (Focus on where you are *now*, not looking back or ahead.)** While I was unable to immediately engage in healing any specific "sore spots," taking that first step toward donning my survivor crown helped stanch the flow of the life essence hemorrhaging from my torn and broken heart. Knowing I would survive this thing called grief dammed up the hole just enough to get me through that particular day.

    I quickly learned how to bring that feeling forward into each new day by focusing on it when I first woke each morning, understanding, yes, I can (and will!) survive this one, single day, and that was the best (and only!) thing I was able to do for myself when the grief was raw and all-consuming. As my mind began to heal, opportunities to work with this important step arose, as you'll see while you move through the coming chapters.

3. **Dig up bones. (Replace old and damaging beliefs with more empowering ones.)** It amazes me even today as I look back over the

first few weeks after Adam's death, to see how I was being shown, as if by unseen forces, how to move forward. It's like someone was whispering in my ear, reading instructions from an invisible *How to Navigate Grief* instruction manual like, "Don't believe everything you hear," or "Never mind what they are saying; what is your gut telling you?"

It would take me some time to develop clear and effective steps for rooting out damaging beliefs, but simply noticing them and asking myself questions like, "Where did this belief come from?" and "Is it really true, though?" was the first step in this process. I was choosing to take that step right away by pushing back against statements like, "It's unnatural for a child to die before their parents," or "A mother never gets over the loss of her child."

What do you see when you look back over your shoulder at your own grief journey? Can you identify pivotal points along your path where you made a conscious choice to think about some aspect of your experience differently? With the hindsight you are gifted with today, can you sort through some thoughts and beliefs that controlled how you experienced your loss? Can you identify one or two specific conversations you had with someone, a book you read, or maybe something you thought of all on your own that ended up inspiring you to survive your own painful journey?

Engaging in things like reviewing your past with the intention of learning something about yourself is not the same as the "living in the past" that folks warn us about. Living in the past is returning to the traumatic event over and over so the horror is replayed again and again within our minds, bringing up all the emotional and physical pain along with it, leaving us breathless and vulnerable all over again while the cortisol and other fight-or-flight chemicals course through our bodies once more as part of an endless, repeating cycle.

Breaking out of a cycle like that begins by simply applying a specific *intention* to your wandering thoughts. The next time your mind wants to drag you back to "that dreaded day," take a moment to say to yourself, "I will allow myself to look at what happened, only this time I intend to find hints and clues about what is keeping me from finding peace and healing."

This way, you make a conscious decision not to go back *into* your story; instead, you *observe* the story. You are taking the reins, announcing your innate right and ability to find healthy ways to heal and grow from anything that comes your way. This is how you begin—you take that first step, and in doing so, claim your own survivor status.

*"Understanding is the first step to acceptance,
and only with acceptance can there be recovery."*

— J.K. Rowling

CHAPTER 2

ZOMBIES CHASING GHOSTS

Since it seemed I would have no choice but to spend my waking hours inside the self-made prison my own mind had become, I decided I might as well pull up a chair and start paying attention to the conversation, my inner dialogue, if you will.

Right out of the starting gate, while composing this letter to my son, I was amazed to realize I had already started working with one of the most important aspects of my grief recovery system, which is to root out old beliefs that leave us feeling depleted and beaten instead of encouraging us to go on.

Looking back, I can clearly see while I had no conscious knowledge or understanding of what exactly I was doing all those years ago and what the lasting result would be, I had instinctively developed the practice of watching my own thoughts play out, sifting and sorting them into manageable piles as if preparing to do the weekly laundry. Good thoughts, bad thoughts, white load, dark load.

But at the time, what to do with the piles of thoughts I had sorted was beyond my comprehension. If you have ever experienced anything close to the shock to your system that news of your child's death by hanging can produce, you would be well aware of how suddenly and completely the mind can blow, frying all circuits and leaving us temporarily cognitively impaired, moving through the world as if in a thick and cloying fog with awkward motions and a zombie-like inability to make decisions or even form cohesive sentences.

It's important to notice the word *temporarily* in the previous paragraph because this impairment to my ability to think, reason, and *remember* was a big threat to my sanity at the time, something I had to claw and scratch my way out of, something I wish others had warned me about and encouraged me by assuring me it was a perfectly normal reaction to such a shock and was, indeed, only temporary. I would have taken great comfort in knowing my brain would heal over time, and my precious memories would return.

Turns out, the effort I made to observe and name my thoughts was easing me into quiet acceptance, something all the experts say we must achieve if we are to recover from the debilitating condition we find ourselves in after a traumatic event. But which steps do we take to accomplish this? Looking back on my story as if watching it unfold through my rearview mirror, I can see the action steps taking shape.

I could not accept what my son had done to himself until I first replaced the beliefs trapping me in anguished confusion, and I was refusing to completely to let those beliefs go. Because even though I could clearly see my son was gone by standing at his grave, fingering the etched letters of his name on his tombstone, once away from that place, I found I could easily slip into a false reality where Adam was "just away somewhere" because, after all, children don't die before their parents. It's unnatural.

Sometimes, these efforts left me feeling drained and exhausted as if I were trying to swim upstream. I'll never say the process of replacing old beliefs is easy, but I will tell *everyone* it is certainly possible if you have a little patience and give it some time. And like me, you will have to decide which sore spots hurt the most and become committed to tackling them one at a time lest you become overwhelmed and your efforts to heal fall by the wayside.

I was also aware, during those first few months after Adam died, that I was simultaneously developing some not-so-good habits I would have to root out later on my journey. One such habit was my self-imposed need to hide certain things from certain people.

I think I took my cues from others when I felt things like shame about spending time wailing over my son's well-used ball cap because it had been on his living body and still carried his signature scent. Since everyone commented on how strong I was and how much better I was handling things than they ever could, I felt embarrassed that behind closed doors I often crumbled into a blubbering mess like when I cradled that hat as if it were Adam's lifeless body. I didn't want them to see me so weak.

Of course, I can see now it was silly of me to feel shame over coveting my son's ball cap. I eventually came to understand it was a perfectly natural way to express love for the deceased and release some of the pain and anguish from my own body.

Everyone will have their own opinions about how the bereaved should behave because we all have differing perspectives about death and grief. While some grow up with a strong spiritual practice that offers them faith that their loved one is in the arms of God and safe from the troubles of the world, others have nothing but TV, movies, overly sensationalized news broadcasts, and the like to form their own images of what a grieving mother might look like.

Regardless of what they believe, judgments are constantly being formed and gossiped about when the bereaved is out of earshot. Make no mistake, we, the bereaved, can sense this happening on some level, and it often complicates our own healing journey, leaving us feeling something is wrong with us.

In addition to keeping the full scope of my pain hidden from almost everyone I knew, I refrained from talking about my budding belief in an afterlife along with my commitment to learning how to communicate with my dead son. That elephant was allowed to stand in the room unaddressed for a very long time, except when those closest to me had enough genuine curiosity to listen intently to my stories of contacting Adam with an open mind.

I was excited but also skeptical every time I thought I was hearing from Adam. In the early months, our contact consisted of pennies found in strange places when I needed a sign or lucid dreams I could always explain away.

I could only share these stories with a handful of people. I will always hold a special place in my heart for those who listened and reacted with the same excitement I felt when receiving such messages. Others would humor me with understanding nods while wearing the telltale look I had come to recognize as the *You poor dear* look.

Over time, I discovered groups who were of the same mind, who spoke, taught, and wrote openly about their encounters with the afterlife.

There I found fellowship based on common beliefs, but I didn't have the wherewithal myself to bring ADCs (after-death communications) out into the public back then—I was just a zombie chasing ghosts.

In this next section of my conversation with Adam, you'll see how frustrating and isolating it is to feel ashamed of your own feelings and beliefs—something a little public education could help change. Isn't it time to allow us to give voice to our *full* expression of grief regardless of what others think is appropriate?

(Dear Adam cont.)

The days leading up to your funeral were a pain- and confusion-filled blur. I remember some family showing up at Leo's place, but I couldn't tell you with any certainty who and in what order they came. Auntie Linda was there, of course, since she had delivered the dreadful news.

If you want to talk about strength, take a look at Aunt Linda's conduct that day. She led and orchestrated the necessary actions families must take after one of their own dies, like having to call your pa and break the news to him immediately after delivering the same blow to me, all without missing a beat or taking any time for herself.

While my recollections of those first couple of days are mostly vague, some are sharp and focused. Hearing Linda repeatedly assuring your father that no, she was not joking, and yes, his son really had just hanged himself is one that always filters to the top when I thumb through the stored memories that were pushed to the back of the closet in my mind for safekeeping long ago.

That moment was heart-wrenching. I could feel his confusion and refusal to accept what she was telling him. All the while, I was wishing I could turn back time so I could save you myself, and then this thing we were being asked to believe would not be true after all.

But true it was, and so I was thrown into an existence I imagine would be like living as a zombie if zombies were real. You see, the news of what you'd done to yourself hit me like a freight train, shorting circuits and frying connections in my brain and nervous system, making it difficult to function beyond the most basic daily tasks.

I was terrified as I realized I had no idea what was happening to me and wondered if I'd ever be able to physically recover. I could have been having a stroke for all I knew. That's how strange it was. It felt like I was watching myself go through everything I had to do, like visiting the funeral home, where it seemed like I was outside the room and observing the proceedings through a window. I was so disconnected from myself that I felt broken in all senses of the word.

The worst came on the day of your funeral when Leo drove me to the church. It was just him and me in his truck, and we simply needed to go straight up Green Street and take a left at the laundromat, but when we came to the first stop sign, I froze because I could not rely on my malfunctioning brain to tell me which way to go so I could tell Leo. I could not find my way to my own son's funeral just three miles down the street in our hometown…the town I raised you in!

This particular memory stings even after twenty years, bringing with it a single tear that comes not from regret and sadness but from deep inside my heart where my most tender memories of you live on. I can still feel the panic rising in my chest that day when I realized my memory had simply been removed. I panicked because if I could forget how to get to the church so easily, was I also in danger of losing my most intimate memories, like teaching you how to drive a stick shift in the parking lot of that very same church when you were sixteen?

The thought of it floored me and was too much to bear. It was almost like I knew I could somehow adjust to not having you here in the physical world, eventually healing from the wound and learning to live without you. But I could not, no, I would not lose my memories of your time here on earth. To do that would wipe you from history as if you never existed, and I simply could not accept that as the end of your story…of our story.

I don't know how I pulled it together that day, but I did, somehow, find the church where your life would be celebrated and your death mourned by those who loved you. And, Adam, everyone loved you. You must have seen how the church filled to capacity, the pastor encouraging the young people who could not find seats to come in anyway and stand or sit in the aisles.

Were you watching from beyond the veil as your bandmates played Metallica's "Nothing Else Matters" one last time together while your beloved drum kit sat appropriately empty and abandoned on stage behind them?

When Pastor asked those in attendance to call out words and phrases that spoke about the person you were, did you hear them as they began shouting wonderful things like "funny," "charismatic," "dedicated," "helpful," "caring," "intelligent," "talented," and "handsome"?

And when a girl from school yelled out, "Great first kiss," which was immediately followed by Jane's own anguished cry of, "Great last kiss," did you go to her, son? Did you go to her then, the young woman you loved so much? Did you go to her and try to wrap yourself around her as she finally gave way to her grief, crumbling there in the church and rendering the rest of the room silent as she openly sobbed?

Was that hard for you? Was it hard to watch your own funeral? To see the fallout of your actions up close and personal? I remember wondering about that then. I felt anxious about it like any mom would be concerned over her child's emotional wellbeing when they were faced with a difficult and painful situation.

You may have died, Adam, but my need to mother you lived on for quite some time, showing up in little ways like the day Leo brought home the stuff you had left in your car, including a bag of dirty laundry he immediately tried to whisk away to save me the heartache of handling your things so soon after your death.

But no, I could not allow him to do the task for me. I had an almost desperate need to wash, dry, and fold them myself before presenting them as final gifts to those who would treasure having and wearing them. I considered that a sacred task, and I cherished every moment, knowing it would be my last act of caring for your physical needs as your mother in this lifetime.

Your well-worn and perfectly curled ballcap I kept for myself, sealing it away in a Ziploc bag, as if I could capture your very essence by preserving sweat from your brow and hairs from your head.

I experienced shame at having your hat hidden away in the back of my drawer, only to take it out when I was sure I was alone. The shame would come in big, crushing waves as I buried my face in the open bag, gulping the scent of my now-dead son like a closet alcoholic who hides while quickly downing a can of beer in seconds, never letting those around them know the truth of their dirty little secret.

I have no idea where the shame came from. Why did I feel like I was doing something wrong? From where I sit now, looking back at the woman who had just lost her son in such a tragic way, my reaction is one of loving compassion for her. I want to hold her and tell her everything will be all right.

I still have your hat in the same Ziploc bag, some twenty years later. But when I open it and breathe it in today, I no longer catch your scent—it has long since faded. I also feel no shame over having it after all these years. I learned to own and even love my personal story of loss and grief somewhere along the way.

While physical traces of you may be gone from that old hat, the act of pulling it out—which happens very rarely these days but always with the same reverence as the act of placing it inside the bag in the first place did—brings me peace and comfort because your handsome face floats before my mind's eye in clear detail every time I do.

It wasn't easy getting to this peace everyone talks so much about, as if once achieved, the pain of losing you would be gone forever. No, I have found that isn't true at all. I still have brief periods of pain after two decades of purposeful grief-healing work. The difference now is I have come to know this pain. I've come to know it so well and intimately that I no longer fight it when it comes. Because I know how it operates, I can see why it shows up when it does, and I can predict how it will move through me. I can now more fully surrender to it. I am no longer afraid of it.

When I release the struggle and offer no more resistance, a peaceful feeling washes over me. You see, the pain, which comes from fondling the memory of the trauma itself, also brings beautiful snapshots of our life together as mother and son, and for this, I have learned to be most grateful. So, yes, pain and pleasure can coexist.

For weeks, I preferred to sleep because you lived on in my dreams. Each time I woke, the horrifying memories of my new reality came flooding in, washing away the last remnants of the beautiful fantasy world playing out in my mind as I slept, the world where you still lived and breathed. It was like you had just died all over again every…single… time. I didn't want to wake up. It was as simple as that. I preferred to sleep.

I didn't know anything about lucid dreaming then. I didn't know you were trying to reach me in some of those dreams. I mean, I'd watch for you during my waking hours, waiting for a sign…a penny, a butterfly, or an unexplained breeze touching my cheek, but I didn't know it was within my power to hone my skills at communicating with the dead. In the years following your suicide, I couldn't help but feel driven to learn as much as possible about what happens when we die.

Looking back, I see how my willingness to open myself to such interactions with you actually facilitated the process itself. While I already possessed a casual belief in the possibility of life after death, I had no idea I could, in fact, continue a relationship with you once you'd seemingly left this world.

But continue we did as you patiently showed yourself to me in so many ways that I have lost track of them over the years. I do remember, perhaps as early as two or three days after your suicide, gazing into the mirror at my tear-stained and swollen face, calling out to you and demanding to know why.

I wasn't asking why you'd killed yourself, but why I was being asked to shoulder this experience since I hadn't understood then that I could and certainly would survive this. And when my own familiar face in the mirror morphed into yours, much like wax melting and then reshaping, I clearly heard your voice inside my head say, "Because you can handle it, Mom." My aching brain grasped for clarification while arguing that what I had just experienced was simply a hallucination and not to be believed.

As time wore on, and I continued to hone my "listening and watching for you" skills, I continued doubting the whole process since most around me were at best skeptical about my encounters and could not offer encouragement for my efforts. Instead, I got more "you poor dear" looks from those too polite to come right out and tell me my experiences and budding beliefs were just wishful thinking from a mother who could not accept her son's death. It was just my way of keeping you alive, they'd say.

But Adam, my interactions with you in your new state of being guided me through that darkness. Like a beacon of light in a night thick with fog, your promised visits gave me something to look forward to, a reason to get up each morning.

I coveted the signs you sent, like the pennies that showed up in the oddest places but always at a poignant and/or relevant moment.

And of course, Metallica songs always get my attention, especially when presented in an unconventional way, like the other day on Facebook. When I opened my laptop to log on, the first thing I saw in my news feed was a video of a pair of figure skaters doing a lovely routine to Metallica's "Nothing Else Matters." So I watched it because…well, there's that "knowing" again. I just know you've prompted this because you know how I love to watch the skaters, and you tied it to Metallica so I'd make the connection and realize it was you popping in to send love and support.

I began to feel immediately. As I watched the beautiful young man with a mop of shaggy dark hair, who could have been you in a different life, twirl and spin and toss his lovely partner around the ice in perfect time to the very same Metallica song performed by your bandmates at your funeral some twenty years ago, my heart cracked open, and I began to weep.

So, yes, Adam, I still hear you. I love it when you send me little signs that you are near, that you are seeing me, and today, I am not afraid to shout it from the rooftops for all to hear.

But in those early days, I kept these experiences to myself, lest those who would judge me would try to convince me they weren't real, claiming it wasn't healthy to believe you were still here with me, and I had to let go.

As a result, I kept my belief in the afterlife along with my litany of "contact" stories safely tucked away from others in my nightstand next to the plastic Ziploc bag that housed your beloved baseball cap—secrets kept hidden, shared only with those I trusted most.

It would take me some time, years really, and a lot more confidence-building experiences before I'd openly share my beliefs with the world at large, come what may.

You see, while I was initially afraid of all those "you poor dear" looks, I eventually came to realize I didn't necessarily dread what people thought of me when they saw me clinging to such theories; I dreaded they might actually convince me these visits were all in my head— wishful thinking from a grieving mother who could not accept her son's death. I was afraid I would be proven wrong, Adam, and that would mean you would be lost to me forever.

But I held fast and true to my studies, eventually finding entire communities who not only believe the Soul continues after leaving the body but also claim we all have a natural-born ability to reach out and interact with the dead in their newfound state of being.

While I obviously cannot prove, beyond a shadow of a doubt, that these signs, symbols, and synchronicities I often encountered were indeed messages from you, I can tell you that following the breadcrumb trail I felt you were leaving me guided me through the most difficult days.

So, at the end of the day, it doesn't matter if science ever finds definitive proof of the afterlife because for me, and thousands like me, simply believing it is truth has saved our lives. Some days I surely would have followed you to the grave had you not assured me that not only were you okay but so was I.

After twenty years, I no longer doubt your messages. I receive them with an open, joy-filled heart. I felt such joy when you and your sister sent me a message the other night as I arrived at Auntie Cindy's Florida house to squirrel myself away for a weekend of writing in a quiet, private space.

I already knew you had heard me throughout the previous week as I called out, stating my intention to dedicate that weekend's writing retreat to our story, asking for your help in getting in touch with all those memories and feelings once again.

On the way there, I told you I would rest and relax the first evening before diving into unpacking our story first thing in the morning. After settling in at Auntie's, I booted up Netflix on my laptop and queued up my beloved *Outlander* series where I had left off. Imagine my surprise when moments later, I realized it was the episode where Roger, one of the main characters, gets hanged!

Really, Adam?

You would think, son, that would have sent me spiraling into the depths of those darkest emotions in preparation for writing the next chapters of my book, but no, my impulse was to simply laugh hysterically.

I felt your presence and approval as I laughed, calling out, "This has your sister's name written all over it. She is here too, isn't she?" At that point, I heard her softly chuckle in my mind.

I was so tickled by the encounter that I just had to share it with both of your aunties since they knew what the weekend was all about for me and would enjoy hearing about it. When I texted them, I was stunned to see the time on my phone was 8:18—your sister's birthday, sending me yet again into a fit of hysterics. She always insisted on credit being given where credit was due!

I absolutely love these exchanges, especially when the two of you "tag team" me like you did that night. But this belief in your continued existence didn't always feel like a healing salve to me. No, sometimes hearing from you only punctuated the fact that I could not reach you, see you smile, or hug you ever again in this lifetime, and when I spent time sitting with those kinds of thoughts, I felt they would smother me.

"How can I say goodbye, when you are still here?"
(Excerpt from the song, "Surviving the Storm" by Vicky Edgerly)

Learning to understand the nature of the Soul and its existence after it leaves the physical body did not stop me from grieving, but it became another cornerstone of my healing's foundation. I had much more to learn if I was to come out of that experience a whole person capable of leading a joyful and fulfilling life.

Since this thing called "death" had taken you, I had an almost uncontrollable urge to follow you, Adam. I wanted to follow you to the grave, not because I no longer wanted to live but because, as your mother, I needed to know where you were and that you were okay. I couldn't stand thinking about you going through any more anguish alone. I needed to see for myself you were not hurting anymore.

Your pain presented the toughest challenge for me. Knowing my boy was so tormented by life he could not conceive of staying on the planet for even one more day brought me to my knees over and over again while I mourned your death. I was living a mother's worst nightmare, one where her child was in unbearable pain, and she was powerless to help.

But in the end, acceptance gave me back my life. Had I not learned to accept what had happened to you was beyond my control, I would never have been able heal my own wounds, eventually learning to grow from the experience.

That growth, brought about by conscious efforts to fully engage with all I was seeing, learning, and feeling, prepared me to weather the storms yet to come my way. Had I known then I would also be asked to bury your sister alongside you a few years later, I surely would have lost my mind for good right then and there.

But life was kind to me, and I was given the precious gift of time. I took that gift and used it. I had no idea how I would traverse the alien landscape I had suddenly found myself in, so I did the only thing I could do—I put one foot in front of the other and began.

Since the dawn of human civilization, many cultures have believed in some form of an afterlife, as is evident by archeological discoveries where the deceased are buried with various belongings, riches, and even food to carry with them into the otherworld.

Today, a little over half the world's population believes in an afterlife of some sort, commonly thought of as "heaven" here in the United States. Yet we still hold back from using this incredibly empowering theory to assist us in our daily lives.

How might believing in a concept such as this help us? The obvious benefit, which you witnessed above in my letter to Adam, is it helps the bereaved come to terms with their sudden loss. Think about it this way: If I didn't believe there was an afterlife, heaven, or something after we die, I would have to accept that my precious boy simply ceased to exist the moment his heart stopped beating. I would have to give him up all at once, "lock-stock-and-barrel," as some would say. Whereas knowing he still exists in a pain-free, light body, with the freedom to learn, grow, and expand to his heart's content in other realms exponentially lightens the burden of grief I must carry. So, it's true. Believing in the afterlife can help some people process their grief.

Note that folks who hold this belief are significantly less afraid of their own death, which is huge in my book since so much anxiety in the world is caused by the subject of our mortality and looming expiration dates. Now that I am in my sixties and approaching retirement, I can attest to this fact. While I do occasionally spend time contemplating it, I do not fear my death, and I have no anxiety about when or how it will eventually happen.

Believing there is more to life than what we can experience while here on earth in a human body sets my mind free to wander and wonder about what my life's purpose really is. It encourages me to look beyond the norm, think differently, and strive to add more purpose to my life while I am here living it—all while understanding I will get to review what I have done here, learn from it, and carry that wisdom into my next life should I choose to reincarnate. Indeed, it makes me a better person because I am more engaged in my life and the lasting, positive effect I can have on humanity, like sharing this story with the world and adding value to public grief support systems.

While my mission is not to convince you or anyone else that we all continue to exist after our humanly death, I need to include evidence of how I used this belief, this *faith* in the afterlife realms to open my mind to new ways of thinking. After all, it was my unwavering need to know "where Adam went" when he died that led me to all the wonderful discoveries I am sharing. It opened both my heart and my mind to allow healing and growth to take place within me.

After-death communication (ADC) with my deceased loved ones is a common theme throughout this book, as you will see as you progress. What about you? What do you think happens when we die? Were you raised in a religion that teaches our dead have "eternal life" and now reside in heaven with God? Have you ever experienced an ADC yourself? If so, how did it make you feel? Were you excited? Scared? Comforted?

If you are curious about the ever-growing-in-popularity practice of communicating with the dead and want to learn more, you'll find a host of information on the web to help you get started. Read books, attend seminars, listen to podcasts, or watch TED Talks on the subject, and you will soon understand what all the buzz is about. Let your own Soul guide you, pondering everything but taking in only that which resonates as *truth* to you. Open your heart to the experience and you'll be collecting your own "pennies from heaven" in no time!

CHAPTER 3

SECRETS ARE FOR SHARING

I still find it fascinating that even while wounded and unable to think beyond our most basic, primal needs, we suddenly and miraculously rebound to rise to the occasion should a loved one show signs of distress. Our innate need to help others overrides our severe discomfort.

By observing this phenomena play out time and again, I came to appreciate the belief that one of the quickest, easiest ways to lift yourself out of depression is to spend time serving others. When we give of ourselves to ease another's pain and suffering, our hearts crack open and our Souls expand. We grow.

While I observed myself doing this immediately after Adam died, I didn't know how I could actually use it as a tool in grief work until years later. At the time, I could do no more than take note of it and spend time wondering what within us makes it so.

I had miles to go before I'd be able to piece any of it together. Moments of discovery like that would flit in and out of my awareness, which was still predominantly a stormy place with only small pockets of calm and clarity. Obviously, I had some hurtles to clear before I'd be well enough to offer any lasting advice or comfort to another in pain.

One of those hurtles was the isolation I felt around people who tried to avoid the subject of death. Those who had been comfortable with me now became anxious and our conversations awkward because they were afraid they'd say the wrong thing. While I maintained empathy and compassion for their struggle, at the same time I felt dejected, left out, and resigned to the fact that my grief was mine alone to deal with and no one was going to save me from it.

Have you experienced this? Even folks living in tight-knit families can feel alone and separated by grief. You would think shared trauma would draw people even closer together. While that is true sometimes, what I see in most families I work with is just the opposite. I see the grief build walls in even the closest relationships. But once you become aware this is happening, it's fairly easy to chase down the root causes and, with a little effort toward authentic communication, it can all be reversed.

Take a married couple who has lost a child, for example. As you can imagine, the grief is sharp, intense, and all-consuming in the beginning. The bereaved parents may have all they can do just to keep their own heads above water, so they simply don't have anything to give their partner by way of encouragement or support. The stress runs high. "Normal" behavior patterns are interrupted, and even distorted so the partners often feel confused or angry about the other's reactions.

One important thing I've learned while working with and observing others is grief is an amplifier. The personality traits you had before the death will be amplified or exaggerated in some way when your life is interrupted by grief. So, if you tend to fill your time with "busy tasks" when you feel anxious or worried, you will most likely try to "stuff the grief" or "hold it in" so you can power through life, filling your schedule with things to do so your mind has no time to linger on the pain of your loss. (We, as a society, tend to see these folks as "strong" or "stoic" when they may really be creating a pattern of avoidance, which in the long run can prolong their grief.)

I fell into this category because my own tendency to want to fix the broken birds and nurse the lost kittens of the world led me rushing forward into a volunteer position helping others with grief long before I had done all my own healing work. While many said my presence inspired others to survive, I couldn't really offer any long-lasting, deep-healing help. I still had much to learn, which could only come through a wider array of focused research and personal experience.

At the opposite end of the spectrum, personalities that dive for cover and hide from the world when uncomfortable things happen might become sullen, depressed, and even take to their beds for a time when the grief is new and overwhelming, allowing self-depreciating thoughts like, *I can't survive this…. I'm not strong enough!* to become embedded in their wounded psyches. Society has taught us to view these people as "weak" or "broken." Actually, both responses simply illustrate the same symptom of grief, which is that your existing personality (along with any pre-existing personality disorders) will be amplified during the acute phases of your grief journey.

Remembering this little fact will help you let go of self-judgement and allow you to begin to understand the reactions of those close to you that you thought somehow "odd" or "wrong." None of these feelings are wrong or inappropriate—they just *are*, and knowing they are considered normal grief responses puts the power back into your hands, allowing you to stop judging yourself and others, and giving you permission to experience and express your grief in all its forms.

The confusion we experience while in acute grief can present in many ways, often taking us by surprise and leaving us wondering if perhaps we are losing our mind. If you've suffered a difficult loss, you may recognize yourself in this next section where I tell Adam how I got through that "year of firsts" by concentrating on one goal or step at a time, never looking ahead or behind but only at the step I was currently on, essentially teaching myself the value and power of "living in the *now*" that all the New Agers talk about.

Another obstacle was my tendency to be stubborn about asking others for what I needed. I not only didn't ask for help, but I become unreasonably offended, discouraged, and sometimes even angry at those who loved me but couldn't see I needed help and didn't offer it without me asking. How dare they return to their lives when mine was still in such turmoil?

One promising thing at the time was my natural ability to find something good in every situation. I have had many friends along my path comment on how I always try to "look on the bright side of life." But where is the bright side when your child takes their own life so suddenly and violently?

While I wasn't yet close to being able to see the gifts this incredibly transformative life experience would grant me, I was beginning to grasp a deeper understanding of how our perceptions can shape reality. Most people seem to have it backward, believing their reality forms and shapes their perceptions. In other words, they assume they are powerless in how they think, feel, and react to things beyond their control happening all around them, believing they had no choice but to feel sad, hurt, or angry.

As I watched my own thoughts toggle between what some might label positive or negative (helpful, empowering thoughts versus damaging, doomsday-type thoughts), I couldn't help but notice how much brighter and more hopeful the world seemed to be when I allowed the positive thoughts to control my mind. While my circumstances remained bleak, my response to them changed according to which thoughts I allowed to dominate at any given time.

I was more acutely aware of this when I observed it playing out in others. For example, when I saw one of Adam's friends light up with genuine joy when receiving something of his they chose to view as a memento to keep and cherish. Others crumbled and collapsed into themselves, viewing the gifted object as a painful reminder of their good friend's untimely death. Taking note of these very different reactions in others allowed me to trust what I was seeing and learning more fully, leading me to the very important revelation that we do, indeed, have a choice in how we respond to anything in our lives.

This one discovery was probably the most important of all because it gave me the key to unlocking the mind-prison I had entombed myself in. To illustrate this, I've chosen to offer my secrets about the full scope of what I was feeling here in these pages. These are secrets I kept from almost everyone I knew and loved back then. They are secrets whose value is only in the telling, because if one thing is to be gleaned from this story, my hope is you walk away with a newfound belief that you have a choice. But before

I share, let me give you a couple of tips to help you begin to understand how you can choose something different for yourself when faced with unnerving circumstances.

While you may not have a choice in what happens all around you, you most assuredly can choose how you accept and surrender to it or deny, fight, and struggle against it. Knowing this, what will *you* choose next time you are faced with daunting circumstances like sudden loss? Will you choose to see yourself as a diamond in the rough as you move through your grief to become someone new, or will you allow your new reality to grind you to dust?

Tips for Getting Started

One of the first concepts introduced in my *Dragonfly Wisdom* (DFW) holistic grief support method, is the ability to exercise your freedom of choice. While others may tell you that you have no choice in how you feel, DFW provides an invitation to explore the possibility that you actually do have a vote in how you respond to your feelings of pain and sorrow.

One way to choose how you will respond is to begin by making simple observations about what you are going through. Take a moment to focus on "the event." Write a brief description using words you are currently comfortable with such as, "My husband John was killed in a car crash."

Underneath your statement of "the event," write one or more statements about how you feel now that this has happened. They might be something like, "I don't know how to go on without him by my side" or "The pain is so intense I don't know how I can live with it."

Now, take a moment to read the statement you made about "the event" and ask yourself this simple question, "Is it within my power to change anything about this event?" Of course, your answer would be no. You cannot change that your husband was killed in a car crash.

Next, read the first statement you made about how you feel about his death and ask yourself the same question. For example, you wrote, "I don't know how to go on without him by my side," so you would ask yourself, *Is it within my power to change anything about this statement describing my feelings?* At first, your mind will try to tell you, *No, I cannot change what I feel or think about this*, but that is not true. *That is the lie we've believed all our lives, and it needs to be corrected.*

With the guidance offered in the *Dragonfly Wisdom* manual, or with the assistance of a DFW facilitator (for those attending groups), along with helpful input from other bereaved participants, you can ever-so-slightly alter your experience by adding the words, "but here I am still standing" to your statement. It would now read, "I don't know how to go on without him by my side…*but here I am still standing.*" Your next declaration could be altered to: "The pain is so intense I don't know how I can live with this… *but I see all around me that others have survived and are thriving, so maybe I can too.*"

This very simple exercise is designed to help stretch your mind around your preconceived notions of how grief is experienced. Two things are happening here. First, you are training your brain to see "the event" as something outside of yourself and, therefore, not in your control. (That helps set the stage for reaching a certain level of *acceptance* about what happened.) This perspective is opposed to your feelings about the event, which reside completely within you and can be altered and shifted at will when you choose to engage in exercises like this one.

Secondly, you are *allowing* yourself to acknowledge and feel the original feelings. Notice I said to add or amend your original thought, not cross it out and replace it. This is a very important point and a common area where holistic trauma-healing programs can fall short or disconnect. They ask you to replace your thoughts with better ones. After much practice and observation, I have seen this fail time and again because the brain cannot make the jump from feeling "bad" directly across the gaping chasm to "feeling good" in one move. It needs some proof before it will take on a new belief as truth. The commonly offered advice, "Fake it till you make it," should not be employed when dealing with deep trauma or heavy grief. Baby steps are called for if you want your efforts to stick.

Through this process, you will begin to see you have a choice. *Finding small ways to reframe the statements you currently believe adds a bit of hope to the story your brain is telling itself.* Like anything, with a little practice, this method alone will go a long way in shaping how you carry your story of loss going forward. Will you continue to carry it as a victim who will never recover? Or will you choose to believe there could be a different way…a better way?

This next section of my letter to Adam illustrates my struggle to find my way through that "year of firsts" that everyone dreads. After hitting a dead end with local grief support groups I faced those birthdays, holidays, and anniversaries without the comfort of community support or guidance. I held on to the hope that once that first year had passed, I would be free and clear of grief and pain like everyone told me I would. Imagine my surprise when I discovered the second year came with its own set of challenges that often left me feeling even worse than I did during that landmark year of firsts.

(Dear Adam cont.)

As I entered what I would later call "the grief journey," which to me signifies a willingness to explore the whole experience, I had very few tools to work with. I had a vague sense of "acceptance" about what had happened and an almost nagging voice in my head constantly reminding me not to take the blame for your actions. Other than that, I was completely blind going into it.

Much like someone suddenly rendered sightless would, I found myself stumbling around in the dark, desperately trying to memorize my new environment and learn from it so I would not continually crash into the walls, thereby causing myself more pain and hardship. And like many before me, I sought help from those who had lived through similar experiences. I needed to see what my survival would look like, what I would look like once I made it to the other side of this life-threatening storm I called Grief.

"We stumble around in the darkness, feeling we are all alone.

Looking for help all around us and seemingly finding none.

Though many have traveled before us, there is no path that's straight and true.

But if, through trust, we open our heart, then surely it will lead us through."

(Excerpt from the song, *"Home" by Vicky Edgerly*)

I decided to try a grief support group. I thought I'd gain valuable wisdom and comfort by being around others in my community who had lived through similar circumstances. I thought that once I was ensconced in such a group, I would find a life preserver, something to hold on to that would keep me afloat and help balance my inner compass, which was constantly threatening to spin out of control and take me down into a place of inescapable madness.

I thought for sure I would receive guidance from those who had already spent time recovering, that they would be shining examples of what I could expect my life to look like once the pain had passed. I thought it would be a place of great learning and healing.

It didn't take long to notice what I would receive from that group couldn't possibly be any further from the lifeline I expected. What I encountered in that first meeting was a room full of people encouraging each other to remain attached to the trauma of their stories by constantly relaying each and every gory detail peppered with commiserating comments from those I would later recognize as "enablers." What I witnessed was simply the blind leading the blind.

But that one experience, hitting a dead-end like that after placing so much energy into hoping I would somehow be saved from this horrible thing, this giant, painful thing with its insatiable appetite for my attention, I see now was the catalyst that started my own unquenchable desire to find a better way through this.

Even amid the fog and cloudy confusion still active inside my brain as it continued its struggle to make sense of the new world I found myself in, a world where children killed themselves, I could clearly see a need for better public education and support when it came to death and grief.

I was absolutely flabbergasted to realize it was 2002, yet I was feeling completely abandoned by my community. I mean, sure, I was surrounded by loving friends and family, especially in the first few weeks after your burial, but the majority of them were simply at a loss in my presence, treading lightly through simple conversations, careful to avoid the taboo subject of you lest I suddenly be reminded of your death.

Of course, such encounters would always begin with, "How are you doing?" to which I would dutifully reply, "I'm okay," to avoid causing them discomfort in the presence of my raw, exposed grief. Except for a very small group of people, this response would inevitably lead to a hasty change of subject, one much lighter that to me seemed completely irrelevant and inconsequential at the time. But I wasn't fine, Adam. I wasn't "okay."

I received many sympathy cards long after your burial, which I came to loath, silently screaming at the people who kept mailing them, insisting I didn't need daily reminders of the immense pain your death had brought me. But when the cards and calls stopped, I was equally hurt that everyone had gone about their daily lives when it was obvious it would be quite some time before I could do the same.

The duality of that one snapshot of my experience seemed to speak volumes to me about how this process would unfold, and so I adopted the belief quite early on that if I experienced pain and chaos during this ride, I could also expect to find pockets of peace and calm. But I never thought I'd be able to feel joy again in this lifetime.

In the midst of such despair, at a time when I had no idea how I was even standing upright, my Soul would step forward and take the wheel. In certain moments, I could literally feel myself leave my body and stand nearby as an observer while someone or something took over my physical form like a marionette saying words I didn't remember thinking and performing actions as if I was running on some kind of autopilot.

The first time I recognized this was the day you died.

When Auntie Linda delivered the news, my thoughts scattered in all directions. I needed to know if it was quick, and I prayed you didn't suffer. I needed to know where you were in those moments, who was with you, and what was happening to you. I needed to know who found you and if you left a note. While my brain worked out its list of important facts I had to learn, my heart was exploding in my chest.

The physical pain became almost too much to bear, and just when I thought I could not survive this thing if it were to become any stronger than it already was, Auntie Linda told me about finding you hanging by your own belt, which you had nailed to the attic access opening in the ceiling of the small hallway where she found herself standing.

She spoke softly, almost mechanically, with her eyes lowered. She spoke of carrying your niece Skyla up the stairs that separated our apartments in the two-family home we shared. She explained, almost desperately, how she called your name over and over but was met only with the unnatural silence that accompanies death. She would later struggle to process her undeserved guilt over turning and walking away to call for help as opposed to trying to cut you down herself, on the off chance you were still alive.

My heart broke into a thousand tiny shards at the realization of what she, my sister, would have to live with. I watched myself shift immediately from my own devastating pain to intense concern for her, and I tried to tell her there was not, nor would there ever be, any blame in all of this for her to shoulder.

I remember thinking, while replaying that conversation in my head hundreds of times in the days and weeks that followed, that it was pretty amazing how I could manage to be so genuinely concerned for her wellbeing when my brain circuits were misfiring and my heart was seemingly broken beyond repair.

It would be days before I could even remember I was supposed to brush my teeth in the morning, yet there I was becoming hyperaware of another's agony and trying to find ways to help them feel better, much like the day of your wake when Greg, one of our closest family friends, could not even enter the funeral home but stood paralyzed outside on the sidewalk until I went out to quietly escort him in.

Or again a few hours later, when your own best friend Ryan could not find the strength to go to your side while you rested on your satin pillow wearing an uncharacteristic turtleneck shirt that hid the bruises on your neck. The horror of it all was clearly written on his face, so I, noticing his distress, went to him, took him by the hand, and encouraged him to walk with me where we knelt together at the side of your coffin.

This ability to have empathy and compassion for others' visceral reactions to your death would become a pattern I would fixate on and use as a tool during that first year or two of my grieving process. Looking at it now, I can see perhaps it was a task my Soul assigned to me to distract me long enough from my own acute discomfort, allowing my mind the time it needed to rest between bouts of thoughts that spun like tornados tossing all the bits and pieces of my life up in the air, some never to be seen again while others eventually fell back to earth but, much like me, were changed beyond recognition.

And while my additional experiences with grief after your sister's demise and Leo's eventual suicide have led me to an even deeper understanding of the universe and our place within in it, my walk through the storm your death brought was a much more arduous one, fraught with many pitfalls along the way that would always catch me unaware.

But as much as those pitfalls seemed to set me back in my perceived progress as I made my way through the worst of it, I can now see how each obstacle actually served to lead me down a path full of self-discovery I would not otherwise have found.

A prime example is my experience with the local support group. Encountering that dead-end planted the seed within me that eventually sprouted into my desire to help others faced with this same type of devastation to find their way through it.

Today, I am looked up to as a source of inspiration and sought out by grievers from all walks of life who each carry a unique story full of constant pain and anguish. Whether through word of mouth or some sort of Divine guidance—I cannot say for sure—they find me. They find me themselves or are led by the hand to my door by a loving friend or family member.

When I sit with each, I can see a thread of common ground stitching us all together. That thread is one that will forever connect us with fellow human beings or bind us tightly, choking the very life from us, all depending on how we choose to see it.

I've chosen to allow that thread to weave its way through time and space touching, soothing, and caressing each individual Soul it encounters. I ride along with it while it completes its task of forming the beautiful tapestry that is my life story. For you see, I've chosen to view this thread as pure gold, one of great value because it has led me to the richest of life's discoveries.

I didn't know it at the time, but what I was doing was choosing to surrender to my experience rather than fight against it. Because I have come to believe when we fight, we create struggle and struggle causes chaos, always bringing more suffering with it. In hindsight, I can clearly see I was guided somehow to a couple of core beliefs when it came to how I would walk through that treacherous landscape I found myself in.

You would be the first naysayer in the bunch as you always fought back when I tried to convince you to "go with the flow." "But what if I don't like where the flow is taking me?" you'd say. I had no good answer back then. I'd just tell you life has a way of working itself out and flowing with it is always a kinder, gentler way to experience the world. Whereas struggling against it requires swimming upstream, exhausting us and depleting all our resources, often leaving us empty and without hope, never any closer to our desired destination.

Honestly, Adam, if you were to look back at your life now, would you not agree with me on this? Because I might as well address the elephant in the room directly and say I think you would still be here today if you had adopted that practice when you were younger. After all, wasn't it your own refusal to accept your circumstances that led you to believe the only way out was to leave the planet?

But I didn't know then what I know now. I only had some vague sense of awareness that there simply wasn't anything left to do but get out of bed each morning and hope the new day I found myself in would be better than the last. I simply decided to survive; that was all that was required of me, which is a good thing because it is all I could manage at the time. My conscious efforts to learn and grow from this traumatic experience would not come until much, much later.

"I will survive, and that's all that's required."

(Excerpt from the song, "Surviving the Storm" by Vicky Edgerly)

I spent many months toggling between waiting for my grief to be over and sitting in a puddle of tears over the latest round of intense emotions that demanded to be released. You see, I joined many in the belief that the one-year mark was some kind of target date on the calendar when I could expect my pain to cease. "The first year is the hardest," they said. "But once you're past all of those firsts, you will be fine," they said. "You will be ready to move on."

Well, I wasn't fine after one year. For me, the second year was harder, but in a different way. I've pondered this again and again over time because even with all the wisdom I gained after losing you, I went on to encounter a similar experience following your sister's death and again after Leo's.

I believe the reason for my continued pain was twofold. I observed how everyone close to me whom I could count on for support breathed a collective sigh of relief once the first anniversary of your death passed and they saw I was still standing. I felt this shift in their perception acutely, and it immediately caused me to feel I was standing all alone in the world, left to carry the heaviest of burdens without support.

Most people I encountered after that magic date suddenly stopped asking how I was doing, falling naturally back into their previous roles of friend, acquaintance, or colleague. It's like they all simply resumed their regularly scheduled program while I was still trying to pick up the pieces of what was left of me and my life, leaving me feeling isolated.

Admittedly, I entertained bitterness and resentment, and as a result, I became stubborn in my reaction and refused to share my sorrow with any of them going forward. I donned a mask of well-being that gave others permission to go about their lives without needing to worry about the state I was in.

But in doing so, I was essentially swallowing my own feelings and burying them in my body where they festered and bloomed into various illnesses, injuries, and diseases I would later have to excavate to finally heal. I may have looked fine on the outside, but I was slowly killing myself on the inside.

Once some time had passed and my brain had healed its damage by rerouting its circuits so I could once again make sense of the world around me, some of the deeper wounds were allowed to float to the surface for attention. One of my defense mechanisms during that year full of firsts was to use those dates as steppingstones I could safely navigate, leaping from one to the next, never looking ahead and not worrying about what would come once the year was up.

I not only lost the majority of my support, admittedly due to my own reactions and how I perceived things (I'm sure any of them would have rallied at a moment's notice at my request), but I also lost those smaller bites of time to set as achievable, survival goals. I felt like I was suddenly standing on the rim of the Grand Canyon, gazing in horror at the indescribable void before me, clueless how to get to the other side, let alone survive the journey.

That's what the second year felt like.

In telling it now, I become more acutely aware of what was playing out within me and can clearly see the blessing of that initial year with all of its firsts. I focused on reaching each of those milestone dates as if they were sought-after levels in a video game. After each one, I could breathe a quick sigh of relief before facing down the next set of perilous conditions I must survive, never looking too far ahead so that I could not see the nightmarish scene of an entire lifetime without you, my beautiful boy.

Was this my own body/mind/spirit's way of protecting itself by doling out the pain in manageable chunks, allowing me to acclimate to shouldering more and more of it until I'd built up enough muscle strength to hold the full weight of it all without collapsing under the pressure? I think it was, Adam.

It's now been twenty years since you left this earth. When the news was still fresh and raw, the wound deep, I remember thinking, *I can live with this for a day, but don't ask me to carry it for twenty-five years!* I couldn't fathom shouldering this burden for such a long time. It was unimaginable. We are taught to believe that—that losing a child is unimaginable.

Over time, my mind did begin to heal, although to this day I do not have the same capacity for multitasking. Admittedly, I cannot do it all simultaneously anymore. I need to chop things up into small pieces lest I feel overwhelmed and become paralyzed like a deer in the headlights, unable to complete even the simplest tasks in a timely manner.

I used to see this change as a weakness, even though many believe multitasking is not something we should seek as an ultimate achievement or measure of our success; it actually damages the brain and, ultimately, the Spirit.

Once again, I found myself acutely aware of how a simple tweak in my perception would save me much suffering, so it was easy for me to feel gratitude for this particular "symptom" of trauma survival. I simply chose to see it as a new "superpower" I'd acquired rather than view myself as damaged or somehow broken.

The takeaway is the new way my brain organizes and prepares me to get things done fosters an approach that allows me to stay in the moment with each task. In this way, I frequently live in a peaceful, almost meditative state—something I am most grateful for acquiring.

When I get agitated while working at something, if I stop and take a step back, I can almost always see my irritation and discomfort is a direct result of trying to do too much at once. So, if I slow down, oddly enough, I get much more done.

Even those who live their lives with a "knowing" (or faith) in the unseen laws of the Universe have moments of doubt and extended periods of "falling off the spiritual wagon," so to speak. Sometimes, insecurities creep in. Some days, we get so involved in the human drama playing out right here on the earthly plane that we completely forget about the bigger picture…the story unfolding behind the scenes at Soul level.

That was certainly common for me back then since I hadn't developed a discipline to help keep me in the flow of things. I often wondered if you were staying with me during my lowest points, like the first time I was left alone after your death. Then I promptly unlocked the door to my heart—which I had bolted shut at the news of your suicide—with a desperate physical need to release the pressure building within me.

Were you there with me, Adam, when I sank to the living room floor and gave voice to the anguish I had held hostage inside the fractured remains of my heart? Did you witness my primal cry of pain to the heavens above, a sound barely recognizable as human but one I would become quite familiar with because I repeated the process after Leo's suicide?

Was it your ethereal hug I sensed, soothing me while I lay curled in a fetal position on the floor that night until all my tears were spent, leaving me in a state of profound peace and connection to all that is?

And was it you, Adam, who whispered, "Not now. Just hold on a little longer," in my ear the day I sat on my bed holding Leo's handgun in my lap? That whisper effectively saved my life as I contemplated the sweet relief of joining you in heaven. Had you literally spoken to me from beyond the grave? I wondered about that while carefully returning the gun to its case—the same gun Leo used to end his own life ten years later, completely unaware of the dark irony of it all.

After all these years, I still get a thrill when I hear from you, Adam. I love the gifts you have been bringing lately. The glorious gift of memories!

And today, even if in mixed company, you will see me standing tall and sharing stories of the silly things you and your sister do to get my attention with the free abandon of any other proud parent spouting off about the antics and virtues of their beautiful children.

And when they see the genuine spark of joy in my eyes, some become curious enough to open themselves to the possibility of exploring a similar mystical path because they want this hope and healing to enter their own lives, leaving lots of folks sort of straddling the middle lane.

(They want to believe in alternative realities where the Soul continues to live after death, but they just can't quite get on board).

If I have gained anything valuable from my belief in and interaction with the afterlife, it's the ability to open myself to infinite possibilities throughout my daily life. I no longer think in terms of "What if it doesn't work out?" Instead, I am more inclined to ask, "What if it does?" And this, Adam, is how I find the "gifts in suffering" that all the poets, mystics, and spiritual gurus talk about.

People who know my story look at me with awe. They all seem to want what I have. They want to live with the same peace, contentment, and happiness I have despite what others see as catastrophic loss and insurmountable grief. They look to me for the secret to achieving such grace after so many traumatic and devastating events.

For years, I saw it as somehow my duty to discover what that secret was so I could share it with the world. I wholeheartedly believed it was my sacred mission to do such glorious work. It'd be right up there with discovering the cure for cancer, a magic bullet the whole world would clamor for.

As unrealistic as that dream was, it did serve me well. For a long time, it gave me something to focus on, something to help make sense of your tragic death and assign purpose to it all. It gave me a reason to keep getting up in the mornings and looking forward to each new day, a gift that evolved slowly over time.

In the beginning, that dream was like a diamond-in-the-rough. It held the promise of great value and blinding brilliance. When I look at it from my perspective now, I see how it also helped guide me through my grieving processes after your sister died and again when Leo shot himself.

How similar our paths were, that diamond's and mine. After all, before it can receive its final round of polishing and reveal it's true inner beauty, it must first be cut. And just like diamonds, people in heavy grief are very different. Some use the pain of those cuts to propel them forward; the need to survive outweighs the desire to give up, while others are simply ground to dust.

The beauty of diamonds is that even the dust particles have great worth and are often fashioned into useful tools. So, I'd say this to the world, "Those of you who have given up, and been ground to dust by the unbearable weight of your loss, please remember you have great value and purpose yet to discover."

I wish you could have seen the brilliance of your shine, Adam, and the truth of your rarity.

CHAPTER 4

FRIED GREEN TOMATOES

Hindsight is a wonderful thing. If only we could access it during instead of after…but then it wouldn't be hindsight, would it? The more I think about it, though, the more I appreciate hindsight is just that—sight we have only when we look back over our shoulder. It allows me to see what I've been through without the intense emotions of the trauma itself. In this way, I can find little blessings and gifts in almost any situation, which brings me to another very important stone to add to the foundation of my grief support system: practicing gratitude.

Earlier, I told you I was watching *Fried Green Tomatoes* when my sister Linda came to tell me Adam was dead and that the movie was wiped from my memory after that mind-blowing news. Well, I'm excited to share how I was recently reintroduced to it and that watching it with hindsight helped me see my "tragic" life story as the beautiful love story it truly is.

I've come to understand that our biggest challenges tend to bring the most wonderful treasures and opportunities to grow, but we cannot see that in the middle of the blinding storm of emotion traumatic events bring. Once I realized that very important truth, I eventually started looking for those gifts every time something happened that made me uncomfortable in some way, with a growing understanding that I already had everything I needed within to see me through my healing journey. I learned to trust myself, and I began to have hope.

Let's see how I employed that budding seed of trust in myself in this next section of Adam's letter, when I tell him about facing the challenge of finding a reputable and effective therapist to help me process everything I was going through. Even today, when I look back with hindsight, I find more things to be grateful for like my innate ability to understand whether a therapeutic approach would be helpful or detrimental during my grief journey. There's a critical point up ahead where you can see this playing out as I choose my own healing path over one recommended by a health professional, glorious hindsight confirming the wisdom of my choice once again.

(Dear Adam cont.)

Much like the grief journey itself, my experience of getting these words down on paper has come with lots of starts and stops, twists, turns, and unexpected surprises along the way. This morning, I woke early in a house on Lake Winnipesaukee that I rented for the week. I've come home to New Hampshire for a bit of a Soul respite. I've come to see family and friends, yes, but also to write. And much like the various occasions where I tucked myself away at Auntie Cindy's house for a weekend of writing, you, Adam, have given me little winks from the heavenly realms to show you are with me and the time is right to put another layer of my story onto the pages of this book.

I wondered during my flight which one of "my three" would come forward. Which would I concentrate on while visiting this beautiful little state where I grew up and raised you and your sister? Memories of you as a child flooded my mind before I even made my connecting flight in Philly, telling me it would be you waiting for me at my private, lakeside retreat, and you did not disappoint your mom.

I felt you there with me the first night as I settled in for some TV before bed. Scrolling for a movie to watch, I was surprised, thrilled, and delighted to see *Fried Green Tomatoes* come up as one of the top five suggestions on the home screen. This was perfectly timed, as always, and helped me slip right back into the story of your life, death, and my journey through it all with you. Thank you, my son. Thank you for showing up like you do and supporting me still after all these years.

I didn't get far, Adam, before I realized just how connected to the characters and the tale our own story was. How appropriate that I start my week becoming reacquainted with it. The way the movie is structured, with the old woman (played by Jessica Tandy) telling the story to the younger character (played by Kathy Bates), resonated deeply. I saw myself in that old woman. I saw how lovely it is to tell a story after many years have passed, allowing the memories to come through wiser, more experienced eyes.

I saw grief expressed in open wailing when the mother lost her son, Buddy, and the opposite from Idgie, his sister, who became quiet, sullen, and distant, seemingly unreachable by anyone or anything.

I watched the patience of a friend serve as a healing tonic, allowing a new life to eventually emerge for Idgie, one full of trial, tribulations, and heroic victories.

I saw myself in the way Idgie found her way back to life by attending to her friend's needs, recognizing how easy and natural it is to jump in to help those in distress while denying our own needs.

The most beautiful observation of all was watching the old woman tell the tragic story with a sense of adventure and a spark of humor in her eyes—it was clear that, just like me, she had learned to love her story. And just like me, her story is one of love and loss, pain and pleasure, death and rebirth.

From where I stand today, Adam, I can clearly see the gifts your death brought me. It was not evident then, mind you. No, I could not see anything good at all about the inescapable torment I was living with in those early days when I would look for you in every young man I encountered. I couldn't see it then.

But today I am blessed with hindsight. Today, I can clearly see how my journey through the darkness, ushered in by your suicide, led me out into the light of a new life. You introduced me to my faith. And like strangers who are destined to become great friends, my relationship with all things spiritual evolved over time, starting slowly as I tentatively dipped my toes in before eventually becoming fully submerged.

It would take Leo's death to finally crack me wide open, but you, Adam, led me to the door, and for that, I will be forever grateful. Thank you, my son.

They say time heals all wounds, but I am not sure time does the healing. Simply sitting still and letting time pass does not ensure it will take our grief with it when it moves on. Believe me, I've tried. That first summer, I felt like I was just waiting.

At first, I was waiting for the shock to subside so I could begin to function again, accomplishing small things like washing dishes or remembering which day to put the trash out. I went through the motions of life, but I wasn't really living. I wasn't fully engaged in anything. I only half-listened to conversations, and it took immense concentrated effort to do things like make a grocery list, pay my bills, and return to work.

I told myself if I just kept putting one foot in front of the other, time would pass and all my pain and the resulting symptoms would simply go away. I got frustrated when it seemed to be taking longer than I thought it should. I judged myself for not healing faster and more completely.

I couldn't look ahead to any point on the calendar, like your birthday or Christmas, with any excitement, but I also did not engage in feeling dread at their inevitable approach. No, I was simply waiting, telling myself what society insisted on—that once I passed the first year, I would be in the clear.

And so, I waited.

And while I waited, I saw you in the young barista handing the woman in front of me her latte. I saw you in the tall, lanky boy with his head shaved who whizzed by me on his skateboard while I walked the streets of downtown Portsmouth, something you and I enjoyed doing together many times over the years. And I saw your animated expressions as you told a fun and engaging story to the person next to you while standing on the corner waiting for the bus. But that wasn't really you, Adam—or was it?

It was hard in those early days to know which signs and sightings were you and which were my grieving brain's way of softening the blow of missing you.

At the time, I had no guidance, no one to help me understand how I was doing in the grand scheme of things. I recoiled from those who would have me believe you were simply gone from this earth, never to be seen or heard from again until the day I entered heaven's Pearly Gates myself, and I hadn't yet discovered the communities of people walking the spiritual path who would eventually celebrate our story as one of everlasting love and life. I felt trapped between something I knew I didn't want and the thing I didn't yet know I could have.

I decided to see a therapist at the gentle but frequent suggestion of those closest to me. Some assumed I wouldn't be able to handle your death or my life without you. They believed no parent could handle such a devastating loss.

I was disheartened to learn, once I got up the nerve to make the call, that appointments with therapists were not easy to come by. It didn't matter that my symptoms were acute and my needs immediate. No, the average wait for a new patient was three to six months, so I settled for the first available therapist, afraid that waiting months would completely undo me.

I was wary but hopeful after the first session. The therapist gave me some homework to complete before the next session. He insisted I must be burying feelings of anger toward you because who wouldn't?

I was resistant, but even so, I convinced myself he was the doctor and knew best, so I tried to open myself to the experience. But in the end, try as I might, I simply couldn't feel any anger toward you.

At one point, I talked myself into believing I "should be angry" at your lack of consideration for your cousin D, who may very well have found you hanging dead one floor above his own bedroom, but I never actually felt it. The closest I came to truly feeling it was when I realized the summer I was so looking forward to with Leo was ruined, tainted by sadness and grief, but I even shut that experience down because I saw it as selfish on my part.

I sheepishly presented my letter to the doctor on our second session, feeling I had miserably failed the assignment. He half-convinced me I was denying my true feelings. Then he pulled out his prescription pad and told me how I could benefit from drug therapy.

My true self stepped forward then and pushed back. "No, I don't think I need drugs. I just need some help in working through my heavy feelings. After all, it's only been two months since my son died."

"Yes, but you said you still cry every day, and it's not 'normal' to cry every day. You're depressed, and the meds will help with that. I promise."

"I really don't believe in taking medications unless they are absolutely necessary. Yes, I cry at some point every day, but I am not crying all day uncontrollably like I was when it first happened."

Still, he pushed his agenda of drug therapy, scribbling away on his pad without really listening to my objections at all. Everything about that felt wrong to me. I mean, I understand that drugs can be very effective for people in dire straits, but my own personal belief is to let the body, mind, and spirit heal as naturally as possible, intervening with chemicals only when absolutely necessary. This was my second visit with this therapist, and he was pulling out his prescription pad before we were halfway through the session!

As damaged as I believe my brain was, it was not so damaged that I'd be swayed by his way of navigating my journey. I smiled dutifully and took the prescription, knowing I would never return or fill the damn thing.

I had a moment or two where I began, once again, to feel completely alone in my grief, abandoned by my community, and now, also by professionals, but this quickly turned into a need to prove the therapist wrong. I had finally allowed my feelings of anger to surface—only the anger was directed at him, not you.

Back then, I couldn't feel gratitude toward that therapist for the poignant life lesson, but I can see the value in it now. Then and there I began to realize I already had everything I needed to process my feelings. I had an internal compass. I had intuition. And the part of "me" I thought I had lost the day you left was still alive and well. I would survive.

I woke to a new day each morning. I had unlimited choices to make, the most important being whether I wished to survive. Once I made that choice, life rose up to greet me, and I began to see glimpses of a brighter world. I began to have hope.

Still, I had to learn my newfound resolve to heal myself didn't mean I had to do it alone. It just meant I didn't have to count on anyone else to heal me. I could, and would, guide myself through by learning all I could, and so I took my time and found a new therapist, one I could interview first to make sure we were a good fit.

I don't remember her name, but I can see her face and feel her gentle presence as she patiently and humbly sat with my grief, gently guiding me once again to the realization I was doing just fine considering all that had happened in my world. I was moving forward.

I think we were about six months out when I started seeing her. I was a bit concerned I might be slipping into denial because I could easily stave off any emotional display when I wanted to, yet I would still crumble into a slobbering mass of jelly if I felt safe enough to let my guard down.

Her approach was so simple yet wise. She asked if I could have put my feelings on a shelf at will six months earlier when the pain was brand new. I had to admit I could not. The intensity of my grief in those early days left me unable to think much of anything, never mind trying to consciously control my emotions.

That little bit of wisdom, that practical example of how I was healing and improving, provided a glimpse into the brighter world that would one day be mine. I would collect these little nuggets of hope and faith and carry them in my heart as I walked forward into my new life. I had lit the fire within that would eventually purge the pain and allow love back in.

I saw this therapist regularly until just past the one-year anniversary of your death. We didn't have a lot to work on, but it was helpful to have someone to check in with. The sessions were a place where I would receive loving encouragement and assurance I would be okay. And that was all I really needed.

One day, she asked me if I had ever heard of EMDR (Eye Movement Desensitization and Reprocessing). This treatment helps process traumatic events involving rapid eye movement exercises. I was willing to try it, so she had me choose an aspect of the event that still haunted me.

By that point, I no longer obsessed over the horror of you actually hanging yourself, and the heart-stopping panic that had flooded my system when I let my mind vividly imagine that scene in detail no longer plagued me.

Instead, I told her about the black-and-white photo I had of you in a little pewter frame. You know the one. You were standing next to the pool at the house on Green Street, and I snapped you as you lifted a hand to your mouth as if to bite your thumbnail, with water dripping down your face and off the end of your nose. I think you were about twelve when I captured that beautiful profile.

I loved that photo dearly, but I was having trouble looking at it because I would fixate on your hands. This obsession was tied to my emotional response at seeing your beautiful body laid out in a coffin where I became fixated on your hands. You see, while the undertaker did a great job with your hair and makeup, you looked like an imposter to me, except for your hands. Staring down at those hands I recognized as yours offered my brain the proof it needed that my beloved son was lying there before me, proof that you were gone.

I assume it was much the same for Pa and your sister. I had needed to see you, even though it was extremely painful to look down on the life-like image of you, void of the spark that had made you *you*. I needed it for closure. Not being there with you when you died, not being allowed to visit "the scene" by the authorities, being unable to hold you while you lay there exposed to all those strangers had been torturing me. I needed to hold your hand one last time.

But when I did, your hand was cold and wooden, a dead thing. The strange waxy appearance, tinted bluish and stiff with rigor, captured my attention in a way that both turned my stomach and held my gaze at the same time.

In the weeks and months that followed, I was brought back to that moment, complete with all the physical sensations, including a queasy stomach, every time I walked by that lovely black-and-white photo of you.

Each and every time, I was transported back to the moment when I had first viewed your body. I offered a silent prayer of gratitude to myself for not giving in to the almost-irresistible urge to pull the turtleneck down off your throat to see your wounds. As your mom, I needed to see your boo-boos.

I'm so very glad I resisted that urge. It would have been a lot harder to overcome the haunting images had I looked, much harder than processing the effect the picture had on me. And I can't help but find it fascinating that ten years later when Leo ended his own life, it would be his hands I asked to see when we went to the crematorium to view his sheet-covered body before incineration—the poetic beauty of the act not lost on me at the time.

In the end, EMDR seemed to do the trick; after one session, in which my therapist had me follow her finger with my eyes while she got me talking about the morbidly captivating "coffin scene," a few unshed tears came up. When I got home that day, I held that picture for a time, inviting the horror and revulsion to come, but I felt only bittersweet sadness over losing you, Adam, my beautiful boy. I didn't have to pack the photo away—it no longer held me trapped in its nightmare, and I was most grateful for that.

To this day, I have no idea why the EMDR session worked. It didn't feel all that powerful at the time, but perhaps my willingness to believe it would help was partly responsible for its success. I really didn't care to know because, again, if it worked, who was I to pick it apart?

I know you've supported me through all the unconventional and often unusual methods of healing I've tried, occasionally leading me to the next modality yourself with little signs directing or encouraging me— like when I was thinking about becoming a reiki master and spoke your name while driving to work, asking your opinion, only to have my eyes immediately lock on a billboard with the giant Nike slogan, "Just Do It." I mean, who could ignore such an obvious sign? I remember the joy I felt in that moment, knowing you were looking out for your ma once again.

We have many healing modalities to help us work through the difficult feelings and bothersome symptoms associated with great loss. Some people seek their doctor's help through medications to calm their nerves and/or help them sleep. Others are attracted to "energy work" like reiki treatments, which can be very calming and soothing, or EMDR sessions with a licensed therapist, which put an end to the nasty trauma-response that held me in its clutches every time I looked at my son's photograph.

Likewise, although I didn't discover this until decades later, it's just as important to address our physical health during times of great distress. Today, grievers have options like yoga classes designed specifically for releasing grief from the body or expressive dance events where participants are guided in soft and flowing dance moves designed to loosen trapped emotion from the body.

If these methods don't appeal to you, perhaps consider deep tissue massage used with the intention of releasing pent-up cortisol and other stress hormones, or a mud bath, a sound-deprivation float tank, or a simple soak in your own tub with Epsom salt, all of which will pull toxins from our tissues and leave you feeling more relaxed and peaceful.

It baffles me that none of these helpful and readily available methods were talked about in the community grief support groups I attended. Unless another attendee brings it up, some might never know these valuable tools are right under their noses. Where were all the printed handouts and/or lists of local practitioners?

Remember, when grief is still raw and all-consuming, our cognitive abilities are hampered, so many seeking solace in a group setting do not have the mental bandwidth to do the research or even make a simple appointment for themselves. This is why I feel passionate about changing the face of public grief support. For starters, I believe we can add immense value to these well-intended groups simply by offering some preprinted materials that highlight all the local services available that folks can take home and review when their minds are calm enough to take in new information.

Even better, community grief support groups would benefit from hosting guest speakers from time to time who can give participants a basic understanding of how the stress and trauma affects their body, mind, and spirit. Offering simple tips and techniques they can take home and use immediately is extremely helpful, which is why these subjects are frequently brought up at DFW meetings, and guest lectures offering demonstrations are highly recommended.

Those who are currently involved with running a group supporting grievers might be surprised to discover a lot of these practitioners will gift their time to your non-profit program as a way of serving others and giving back to their communities. These suggestions among many others can all be found throughout my *Dragonfly Wisdom* manual and would be a valuable addition to your efforts to support those in this kind of pain.

To recap: You can start your own self-care protocol by googling any of the following terms to find practitioners in your area. Then attend the sessions you feel most drawn to. Your body will thank you. I promise!

1. Yoga for Grief
2. Dance/Movement Therapy for Grief
3. EMDR Therapist Near Me

4. Reiki Practitioners Near Me
5. Trauma Touch Therapy
6. PTSD Massage
7. Somatic Massage Therapy
8. Myofascial Release Therapy

CHAPTER 5

FOLLOW THE SIGNS

Though it was in my nature to look on the bright side of things, I didn't yet know how I would survive the emotional storm I found myself in. What I did know was I had a choice.

I could assume the experience would be devastating and leave me and the life I had known torn to bits like wrecked beaches after a hurricane. Or I could choose to hold on to the hope that once the storm passed, I'd find a brand-new world full of exiting opportunities to build a new life, one of my own design.

As I wrap up this letter to my son, you'll see how everything I was learning and experiencing along the way strengthened my faith in myself and enriched my life. I hold so much gratitude in my heart for Adam. I'm grateful to have had that special little boy with his silly, entertaining antics, and the handsome, moody young man the whole community adored call me Mom for the eighteen years he walked the earth, and I'm grateful now to have his support and guidance from beyond the veil.

Though it may be hard if you are in acute grief to understand how I could possibly have such an attitude toward my experience, I can promise you it is quite true. I can also assure you it didn't come easy, but it was something

I developed and grew over time. My growing ability to experience Adam in his loving and wise body-less form, his true Spirit essence kickstarted my desire to change my perception of the world around me.

The various signs and messages Adam delivered after his death were precious to me, offering hope and encouraging me to keep moving, searching, and reaching for something better. In this way, his death became my teacher and my savior. His death taught me how to live.

While teaching folks to communicate with the dead is not a module within the Dragonfly Wisdom grief support program (group facilitators are not psychic mediums), we do offer simple techniques people can try on their own that introduce the process in Phase Two meetings. In addition, we allot time for open discussion about ADCs (after-death communications) where participants are encouraged to share their personal experiences with the group.

For now, if you are at all curious about how ADCs work, I recommend starting with the book *Hello From Heaven!* by Bill and Judy Guggenheim. The authors have been conducting intensive ADC research since 1988, and this best-selling book is packed with stories of after-death contact experienced by everyday folks from all walks of life, with all manner of spiritual and/or religious backgrounds. It's a true testament to how simple the process really is and how prevalent it is within even the most conservative societies. We may not be talking about this in public (*yet!*), but when it comes up in an open forum full of others with similar experiences, the stories come pouring out. The book is available at most bookstore chains and on Amazon. Give it a try. You have nothing to lose—and blessings beyond measure to gain!

(Dear Adam cont.)

I love all the signs you continue to send me, Adam, and how creative you can be in getting my attention. Although I don't seem to hear from you as often as I do your sister these days, I still get a thrill every time I do. I also love how completely I now know when it's you instead of looking for proof or asking for more evidence like I used to.

It doesn't always happen instantaneously here in earthly time, but if I express my wish to hear from you and then just let go, as in relax and forget about how or when you'll turn up, a magical encounter is sure to follow soon, often taking me completely by surprise, which makes it taste all the sweeter when it arrives.

This easy, comfortable way of communicating with you has evolved quite a bit from the early days when I doubted every encounter. While my faith and ability to hear you has grown immensely since then, I still hold some of the first contacts close to my heart, crisp and clear in my memory, like the vivid dream Leo had just a few days after you left this earth.

I had told him about our family friend Lea, who had passed after a long battle with cancer, but he had never actually met her, so it surprised us both when she came to him in a dream instead of coming directly to me. She told him very pointedly he was to wake up and give me an important message. He was to say these words exactly: "Don't worry; it's like living in a candy store!"

He woke in the wee hours of the morning, fresh from that encounter, and offered me that very first lifeline…the one that allowed me to begin to trust the theory of the afterlife and relax in the knowledge you were safe and apparently enjoying your newfound state. What kid wouldn't want to live eternally in the wonderous world of a candy store?

I cannot help feeling grateful for how much I have learned from this whole experience, Adam, but if given a choice, I would still have you here with me physically. You'd be in your forties now, and I sometimes wonder what it would be like to have you in my life.

I imagine you would have a family and children with your thick, curly, brown hair and your tendency for the dramatic. Or maybe one of your kids would have your musical abilities, enjoying a career as a singer, songwriter, or musician.

Today, I enjoy listening to women my age talk of their grown children, a son who helped them install a new dishwasher, or a daughter who took them to lunch. Hearing these accounts and meeting these vibrant, living offspring used to hurt, but somewhere during my healing journey, I turned that around to where I genuinely enjoy them. The proverbial "living vicariously through another" phrase comes to mind.

That wasn't always the case, though. I did struggle a bit at first with the fact you didn't bring children into the world, wishing there was a "mini you" I could hold on to by way of keeping you alive. But once I started making conscious efforts to understand how my thought patterns affected my ability to enjoy life, I changed my perspective to one of gratitude that no children were left behind to try to make sense of what you had done.

Processing a parent's suicide can be particularly challenging, no matter how old the kids are at the time of death. Children have a tendency to assume blame for their parents' actions and often allow their minds to wander round and round through heavy thoughts like, *Why did they leave me? Was it something I did? Am I not good enough? Why didn't they love me enough to stay?*

Unless such kids have someone to counter those damaging thoughts, continually reassuring them it wasn't their fault by offering truthful, age-appropriate explanations for why Daddy or Mommy chose to go, the misplaced guilt can become embedded, shaping their view of themselves and the world, limiting their ability to enjoy life and tainting relationships because they have a grieving and guilt-hardened heart.

These early observations propelled me forward each day, easing my discomfort little by little. While I obviously fared quite well given the odds against me, others in my circle did not.

Losing you was undoubtedly the hardest thing I encountered to that point in my life, but I was not so self-absorbed that I didn't notice the pain others went through, although most tried to keep it from me as if my own anguish should somehow take precedence over theirs. Even then I thought their pain was just as relevant and important to understand.

As I said before, I spent a lot of time reading about grief. Most of the information simply sifted through my wounded brain and leaked out the various cracks and gaping holes that the shock of your suicide created, but one particular book stuck with me: *When the Bough Breaks:*

Forever After the Death of a Son or Daughter by Judith Bernstein. It takes the reader chapter by chapter through the various relationships the deceased might have had with those left behind.

The chapter about grandparents offered me a glimpse into what my mother and father must have been going through. I saw through their eyes that while they grieved for you, their grandson, their deepest sorrow may have been the anguish over watching me, their child, enduring so much pain. This look inside others' journeys allowed me to soften my reactions to people's behavior.

Take your sister Tierra for example. In the first few days after your suicide, she stayed close to me, quietly supporting me and taking part in all the preparations for your funeral, including going through old photos to make a nice poster board for the mourners to chat over during the wake.

Once the required ceremonies were over and we saw you to your resting place—the old cemetery with its rolling hills, ancient stone monuments, and century-old shade trees—she took your niece, Skyla, and went back to her life with her new man, Jerry, in Connecticut, contacting me very little the first couple of years.

I called to check in from time to time, but she really didn't let me see the scope of her grief. She kept it hidden from me, probably out of some sense of duty to be strong for her bereaved mom, whom she believed could not survive the burden of watching her surviving child struggle with so much misery.

For years, we kept our conversations light, sticking to her kids, family events, and occasional requests for old family recipes. We didn't begin to find our way back to each other on a more intimate level, eventually healing our relationship, which was so strained while she was growing up, until she called to tell me she had cancer.

It was six years after your suicide. At the time, I was aware Tierra was chronically depressed, most likely a result of unresolved grief over losing you, her only sibling. But I couldn't reach her then; no, she wasn't letting me in at all. She didn't let me in until her illness. Once faced with such a frightening future, she decided she needed her mother.

After her initial surgery and radiation treatments, Tierra, admitting that her relationship with Jerry wasn't working out, packed up your nieces and nephew, and came home to me to rebuild her life—we still had hope she would beat the horrible disease.

Once she settled into their little place an hour north of me, she finally shared her truth about how your death affected her. She spoke tenderly about how difficult the first year was, admitting she barely made it out of bed or off the couch most days—the grief was all-consuming and debilitating.

Tierra ached for you, feeling her life's essence had gone to the grave with you. She talked about being blindsided by your death over and over again—every time she reached for the phone to call you with something newsworthy, forgetting for a moment you were gone, only to have the truth, sharp and cutting, come to her again and again.

When her illness advanced to the terminal stage and she was putting her affairs in order, she shared even more. She gifted me her "Adam box"—a little wooden box she kept a few mementos in, like your wallet, a guitar pick, and your name badge from your job at Olympia Sports.

That box contained a poem she wrote expressing how things were for her as a young woman living in the aftermath of her beloved brother's suicide. Even though I am quite sure you must have been right there with her as she poured her heart along with her tears onto that page, I want to share it with you here, as a way of threading our stories together.

Some Days

by Tierra Lynne Brewster

Some days I just want to crawl in my mother's womb, because there, I knew I was safe, sound, and without worries.

Some days I want to cry for my loss, but no tears are shed; others I cry and feel more lost than I have ever felt in life.

Some days I don't want to get out of bed for fear my mind will awaken, and I will have to remember everything.

Some days I want to wake up fresh, happy, and enjoy my day, but constant reminders of him put me at a standstill.

Some days I want to scream at him for what he has done; others I want to scream at myself for what I didn't do.

Some days I want to die myself, forget everything, and have no more problems; then I realize that could never be.

Some days I wish I was my daughter and full of innocence, without worldly cares or concerns, and was happy always.

Some days I want my daddy to hold me and tell me everything will be okay, and it will be because he said it, so it's true.

Some days I hold my own child and tell her everything is going to be okay, and she believes me even when it isn't always so.

Some days I stare blank-faced at his picture and try to figure out what was going through his mind and what he was feeling.

Some days I feel selfish that I'm the only one left and all attention is on me when it should be used on people who need it.

Some days I feel alone because I'm the only one left and everyone's attention is scattered and there is no time to heal me.

Some days I cry, some days I crawl, some days I grieve, some days I fall, some days are good, some days are bad, and some day…

I get to see him again.

I still feel the weight of her words deep inside me when I read these verses. She captures quite well how fractured we all felt after you left, as if part of our own bodies were violently torn from us. Some emotions felt like storm surges threatening to drown us one moment, then numbing us so we felt nothing the next.

I also learned during Tierra's long, drawn-out illness that joining you in the heavens was her secret wish all along. At one point, she confessed a desire to follow you to the grave. She spoke about longing to take her own life for years after your death and confessed feelings of anger toward you for having taken that choice away from her. You see, she simply could not saddle her parents with the crushing weight of grief that would surely come after losing both children to death by suicide.

I remember wondering then if she was somehow creating the cancer to make her exit without technically taking her own life. If I've learned one lesson to hold on to through all of this, it is to have absolute faith that my Soul is in charge and knows exactly what it is doing when it leads me to my most memorable experiences. Knowing this gave me peace of mind enough to know her Soul was indeed leading her to whatever awaited as yours had for you, my beautiful boy.

As I come to the end of this letter, I am brought back to a memory I've held close inside my heart since you were five days old. It was 2 a.m., and I had just gotten you back to sleep after a late-night feeding and two-hour stretch of colic. While gazing down on your sweet, little, cherubic face as you dozed fitfully, my twenty-one-year-old self was suddenly gripped with the horrifying realization you were going to "die young."

While my mind tried to deny what I felt and explain it away as some sleep-deprived dark fantasy, my heart knew it was true. As I stood there by your crib, I experienced the same kind of panic that news of your death some eighteen years later would bring, and so I grieved, hot tears quietly streaming down my face while your father and sister slept peacefully, unaware in their rooms nearby.

I learned later this type of "premonition" is common with parents who have lost children, and I have run across many similar stories of a mother or father somehow "knowing" they would outlive their child.

In my case, I chose not to fixate on that one night of knowing, eventually letting it filter down to the bottom of my pile of memories—still there but never taken out to look at in the light of day. But since you grew up with needing frequent trips to the emergency room to get stitched up or have broken bones set, that old knowing tried to force its way to the forefront of my awareness from time to time, demanding attention.

I suppose things could have been a lot different if I had let that late-night episode dominate my thoughts as you grew up. If I knew what was coming, I would have surely gone insane with worry or driven you bonkers trying to keep your active little self bubble-wrapped and safely tucked away at home all the time.

I am thankful I did not make life scary for you in that way by not letting you spread your wings for fear of a pending accident. I can rejoice knowing that you lived with an adventurous Soul for the short time you were here, and I did not dampen your spirit or stifle your creativity.

The experience of losing you, only to find myself has brought so much meaning to my life. I now look back and wonder how that woman managed to live the first forty years without such faith in herself and the world around her. It's like I was sleepwalking in a black-and-white world, going from day to day without any purpose other than getting by and caring for the needs of those I loved, aiming for the finish line— my own death.

By contrast, I now move through a world full of brilliant colors, finding purpose in every mundane task, understanding my every thought, emotion, and action will help shape the world around me. The discovery of things like being able to choose how I feel about something and our innate ability to alter what we believe have freed me to live a much more engaged life.

As I walk forward into retirement here on this earth, I no longer look ahead, half-dreading, half-longing for my own death, the day I can hug you again. Instead, I daydream about all the fun, learning, expanding, loving, and giving I can fit into the time I have left. I do this without worrying over when my time will come because I know you and your sister will be there waiting for me. Meanwhile, each and every day here is still exciting, offering someone new to meet, a challenge to conquer, or something enthralling to engage in.

So, I thank you, my son, for all you've led me to see, experience, and discover. I thank you for my newfound confidence in myself, my ever-expanding understanding of the Soul's journey, and my growing faith, which sustains me through thick and thin. I thank you, Adam, for my very life.

Great value is found in writing love letters to the dead. You can see how writing this one to my son now that I am in my sixties has served me by uncovering more opportunities to heal buried layers of my story, like realizing I had lost all memory of the movie, *Fried Green Tomatoes*. You've also learned a bit about who I am by watching my reaction to that little tidbit of information. I confronted that revelation head-on, watched the movie again, and was floored (and touched!) by all the synchronistic connections (I have learned to call them *God winks*) as I recognized parts of myself in some of the characters.

I hope sharing these very personal letters will help you in your quest to understand the grief journey and find healing after your own loss. I showed you it is possible to "find the gifts" in a life-changing situation like this. You've watched as I moved from a confused, somewhat broken woman to a seeker of knowledge and truth after refusing to believe what my society told me—that there is no coming back from the death of a child.

To this day, I am unsure what the most effective driving force was in all this. What propelled me forward to carve out my own system of processing grief in healthier ways and sharing it with the world? I think my need to find purpose in my son's death was sharing top billing with my innate will to survive. At any rate, the result was almost magical because I truly did cross a threshold into a brand-new world where parents can *choose to thrive* after such a tragic loss. Using newly discovered tools like meditation and purposeful breathwork to help calm my anxieties, and diving into studying all things metaphysical and spiritual served me quite well, laying a foundation for the work yet to come.

While I gained some wonderful insights into the human condition and the nature of the Soul in the years after Adam's suicide, I was still somewhat fragile and, luckily, unaware of the next tragedy heading straight for me in the form of my daughter's cancer. But as you will see in the coming chapters, I once again made a conscious choice to lean into the experience with a mindful effort to allow it to unfold and shape me into someone stronger and maybe even a bit wiser. After all, we can't really *transform* grief like some would suggest, but it most assuredly will transform us, whether or not we want it, so why not take an active role in the process? Doing so gives us the power to direct and shape the transformation.

How will your grief experience change you? Who will you become? Will you be emotionally stronger because of it? Will you adopt a "live each day to the fullest" attitude? Will you become sullen and withdrawn, closing your heart down to protect it from feeling this kind of hurt in the future? Or, like me, will you don a new sense of fearlessness because (after all), the worst thing imaginable has already happened and you survived, so what could possibly feel worse? The possibilities are endless; our choices are abundant.

Let's see how I do when faced with losing my only remaining offspring in the next segment of my story of transforming through loss. But first, I'd like to teach you a simple breathing technique I found helpful in calming my nerves when my mind tried to conjure up Adam's death scene and the panic rose in my chest, threatening to undo me completely. Many conscious breathing techniques, available on the internet, are designed to help calm the *vagus nerve* or *parasympathetic nervous system*, and they can be very helpful during a trauma response. If you search the terms mentioned above, you can try other techniques until you find one that's right for you. Here is my personal favorite because it's effective and easy to remember.

Breathing Exercise: We have a tendency to hold our breath or hyperventilate when anxiety rises too high or during a panic attack. Simple, controlled breathing techniques are quite helpful and can go a long way in calming the body's physiological responses to stress and trauma.

What do breathing exercises actually do for us? They immediately interrupt the rising panic by giving our brain a finite point of focus (intentional breath counting), and they flood our system with precious oxygen, which is typically limited during high stress and anxiety. This response allows our bodies to feel less threatened because we can calm and relax ourselves (deep-belly breathing).

Remember the following two important things when employing this method:

1. **Make sure your inhaled breaths are pulled deep down into your belly.**
2. **Make sure your exhaled breath is *longer* than your inhaled breath.**

Because it is so simple, this method is my go-to for supporting the newly bereaved or someone experiencing acute grief who, typically, will not have the conscious ability or physical energy to learn new things or do daily exercises. They simply can't until they've had some time to heal, which makes this a wonderful tool to offer folks participating in Phase One of my *Dragonfly Wisdom* program.

The exercise goes like this:

A. Place your hand on your belly so you can feel it expand and contract with your breath.

B. Breathe in slowly and deeply, pulling it down into your belly, feeling your abdomen expand. Try doing this to the count of five.*

C. Hold the breath for the same count as the inhale. (In this case, five.)

D. Slowly exhale, expelling all the air and feeling your belly contract. Exhale for the count of eight.

E. Repeat as needed until you achieve slow, regular breathing. (Typically, three to five rounds will do unless your symptoms are severe. Conscious breathing techniques will not hurt you, so you can repeat these steps as often as needed. The beauty is it can be done anywhere at any time!)

*The exact number of seconds you inhale, hold, and exhale is not important. The only two things you need to do for this to be effective is pull the breaths deeply into your abdomen and ensure you exhale slowly so it lasts at least a few seconds *longer* than the inhale.

"The boundaries which divide life from death
are at best
shadowy and vague.
Who shall say where the one ends,
and where the other begins?"

— Edgar Allan Poe

PART TWO

TIERRA

CHAPTER 6

WHAT WE SEEK WE SHALL FIND

Some say an expected death brings kinder, gentler grief than sudden, unexpected death does, but having gone through both, I think that's a matter of opinion. To me it's like the difference between peeling a Band-Aid off slowly or ripping it off quickly. Both are painful. One is sudden, intense, and all-encompassing while the other is excruciatingly slow and drawn out but less sharp. Which do you prefer?

While news of Adam's suicide was unexpected and shocking, throwing me into a sink or swim mentality, my daughter's slow decline and death by increments introduced a whole new set of emotions I didn't think I was prepared to deal with.

Even so, the *gifts* in my experience with Tierra, whom I refer to by my pet name for her, "Dawtah" (spoken with a long, drawn-out fake English accent) throughout my letter, floated to the forefront of my mind immediately. That we had time together to somehow prepare for her departure was something to be grateful for from the very beginning, so I grabbed that gift and held it close.

Recognizing I could choose how I would think and feel about our circumstances, something I discovered while grieving Adam's death, also came into play early in my daughter's story, quickly becoming a regular practice for me as I moved through the experience.

Opting to look for the gifts Tierra's long illness would bring us was a choice that helped sustain me through the two-year process. Accepting the sudden death of a child is one thing, but walking your kid to death's door with grace and purpose is quite another.

Practicing my newfound methods of staying in the moment and choosing to find little ways to feel better about what was happening was effectively staving off most of my anxiety, but I was at a loss when it came to helping her calm her own fears. I needed help.

Tierra's chosen path in life was a difficult one. She often leapt head-first into new relationships with friends and lovers, giving her heart away quickly and completely, the objects of her affections not always capable of reciprocating. While she was growing up, it was hard for me to watch various friends take her adoration and use it to their advantage until they got bored with her, only to toss her aside ruthlessly in favor of another, more popular friend.

But motherhood has a tendency to change women, helping them grow stronger and more self-confident, and my daughter was no exception. In the handful of years she spent living in Connecticut and then New York, she went on to have two more children with Jerry, the man I believed she loved even though they struggled to keep their relationship together at times.

When she first came home to New Hampshire with her three children—Skyla, RyLee, and Qwynn—in tow, she was determined to leave Jerry behind in New York and build a new life for herself and the kids with my help. She had just completed her surgery and radiation treatments in New York and was full of optimism about her future.

But the reality of her grave situation set in as it became obvious to everyone that her health was not bounding back. Her worries over what would happen to her children if she were to die were demanding her attention so she made efforts to mend the broken relationship with Jerry, eventually inviting him to come to New Hampshire and reunite with the family.

Tierra's children were always more important to her than anything else in her life, which was why, immediately after being pronounced *terminal* by her team of oncologists, she made arrangements to come and live out her hospice days with Leo and me once she became too sick to look after herself. She didn't want to burden Jerry with caring for her needs, which would inevitably distract him from the needs of their children and the household. But her main reason for wanting to die at my house was to save her children from living with the daily suffering that was bound to get much, much worse. She wanted them to be free to be loud, noisy, and messy kids without the added stress of having to tip-toe around a sick mama in their daily lives.

By the time I settled her into the room Leo and I prepared for her in our home, I had developed a passion for spiritual study and had a particular interest in Shamanic work. Historically, a Shaman would be present in Indigenous communities throughout the world, some acting as religious leaders or priests while others used Shamans for physical healing. Shamans often have great knowledge of the tribe's history and claim a connection to the spirit realms through the common practice of "journeying." Journeying is reaching an altered state of consciousness through various methods such as deep meditation, chanting, dance, ritual, and ceremony. Once in an altered state, they are seen to commune with the ancestors and other benevolent beings of Spirit who offer support and guidance for all of life's challenges.

While I chose to use metaphysics as the vehicle to deliver my emerging grief healing methods, the tools themselves do not require an attachment to any particular spiritual or religious belief. I was merely taking some very simple activities, shown to calm the nerves and reduce fear and anxiety by rewiring the brain's way of thinking (perceiving!), and wrapping the whole thing up in a package that appealed to my sense of adventure. Simply put, discovering the world of Spirit and metaphysics lit a fire of excitement within me that breathed light and life into a story full of death and despair.

One of the first things I did for Tierra, once I had her settled in for her end-of-life hospice care, was to bring in a Shamanic practitioner to offer insights into her journey with cancer. I believed this medicine woman would be able to give my daughter a deeper understanding of what her Soul had planned for her in this lifetime, hopefully, helping her more fully accept what was happening.

The experience did not disappoint us. We learned so much about our relationship as mother and daughter, which helped us relax into a comfortable state of forgiveness, release, and unconditional love. I also witnessed the stunning beauty of the moment when a suffering human recognized the essence of her own immortal Soul for the very first time, a blessing I will cherish forever.

I was grateful for this woman, who broke through Tierra's med-hazed mind with its fast-moving, often disjointed thoughts and worries, giving her something fascinating to focus on, something that left her feeling good about herself and her choices, giving the short life she was living more meaning and purpose.

While this one encounter did not completely remove Tierra's daily anxieties, it did make a lasting difference to her emotional comfort, which I noticed recurring every time we talked about that day. In the nine months I cared for her at home, I employed other Shamanic techniques, engaging in rituals and ceremony to foster a bond of togetherness within the family.

We made a ceremony of creating a beautiful memorial by placing Tierra's handprints in cement alongside the tiny impressions her three small children had made. We stood in quiet reverence as she placed crystals, stones, and other objects that spoke to her life and personality into that cement slab we'd later place in her memory garden on our property.

Once Tierra was gone, her children and I made it a ritual to visit that spot and, much like we did at her gravesite in the local cemetery, place small gifts of stones and feathers along with prayers of love that served to keep her memory alive and help us all feel deeply connected to one another.

Mother and daughter relationships can be somewhat enigmatic. They tend to form in one of two ways. We either become super-close, almost inseparable as we share confidences only another woman could truly understand, or we go head-to-head against each other, living in a constant power struggle as a battle of wills plays itself out time and again. My relationship with Tierra was the latter. She and I struggled to get along when she was young, and at times, I don't think we liked each other very much.

I suppose that was the first elephant in the room to note in our story— we didn't seem to like each other. I mean, who among us would actually stand up and say so in public, even though many of us live it in our daily lives? Once again, I am reminded of all the things society tells us we *should* think, feel, and do, completely negating any thoughts and feelings that don't fit the mold.

This rocky relationship with my girl must be told to serve this book's purpose. You see, many circumstances arise when it comes to processing grief, so there is no one-size-fits-all solution. I have encountered hundreds of people in various stages of grief over the years, and I have learned that unresolved relationship issues can complicate the healing process, often holding us in a pattern of guilt and regret over missing our chance to repair the bond before a loved one dies. My daughter's terminal illness gifted us such a chance.

Dear Tierra,

Well, Dawtah, you seem to be everywhere lately. I've been feeling your presence all around me these last few weeks. Getting little signs and signals you are near is always a treat, like suddenly noticing your birthdate displayed on a clock or my phone not once but often twice a day.

It's funny how as a kid you were belligerent in your refusal to conform to my wishes (a.k.a. clean your room, do your homework, stop lying, and other horrible things our mothers try to visit upon us when we are young), yet now, in death, your role is more of taskmaster. I love it, though; the guidance you bring is always appreciated, and the encouragement you offer when I'm struggling with something is priceless.

It's interesting how our relationship dynamics changed once the cancer had finished with your body and set you free. It's also interesting how quickly I was able to understand and accept what was happening. I mean it's so much easier now simply to let you take the wheel and guide me than it was to stand by and watch you make decisions I knew would bring you heartache and hardship while you were here living among us.

Now, more than a decade after your transition, I realize how many beautiful insights into the Soul's journey your illness and death brought my way. It's true, and I know you are happy I feel this way about it. It was still hard to go through. Everyone says an expected death is easier to mourn than a sudden, unexpected one. I believed it, and to some extent that certainly was true for me, but in other ways…not so much.

Your story came with so many hurdles, challenges, and roadblocks, all leading to its inevitable conclusion with death as the final prize, that it was quite shocking to find "the gifts" in the whole experience. When I first heard of the theory that difficult experiences present our very best opportunities for learning and growing, I wanted no part of it. I would have been perfectly content living a less-than-exciting life of certainty and comfort. Who wouldn't? Who on earth would choose turmoil and hardship for themselves over safety and surety?

Eventually, I came to understand the wisdom in seeking out little gems, gifts, or lessons hidden within any challenge or trauma. The "gift" is typically a new belief or strength we gain because of said challenge, but the real treasure is the act of looking for it. The way I see it, the moment we decide to go looking for something to be grateful for in the middle of a crisis, we've made the choice to lay aside victimhood and don our survival crown. In other words, what we seek we shall find.

All I needed to do was pay attention to what I was seeking. Not easy when sadness and sorrow engulf your whole being. Not easy, no, but certainly possible. In my darkest hours during your illness, I simply kept reminding myself it was, indeed, possible.

While the grief after your brother's death came on fast and strong, my grief over losing you happened slowly over time. Cancer may have taken your life, but it brought us months of beautiful mother-daughter time. Time you and I needed to heal our troubled relationship. Time I wouldn't give up for the world, although I would have traded roles with you in a heartbeat if given a choice. That was the first gift I noticed from the experience—the gift of Time.

Then there's Choice, another concept I never understood until faced with so much loss. No one told me I actually had a choice in how to handle my grief. In fact, just the opposite was true. People were telling me constantly how unusual I was because losing a child should have killed me. And here I was about to lose my second and only remaining offspring. How would I even survive, they wondered. "By choice," I said. That's how I would survive—I would choose to.

I know you never understood that. You insisted you didn't have any choices when it came to how you felt about something. But I've learned that simply isn't true! Of course, the body and brain have their own physiological responses, like releasing the stress hormones cortisol and adrenaline when something startles or frightens us, but once those fight-or-flight chemicals are spent, we really do have an opportunity to turn things around. Once we see there is no imminent danger, we can slow down and purposely look at how our situation or recent events left us feeling.

Out of necessity, I developed a ninety-second rule. Whenever I felt my heart racing and panic rising over your impending death, I would wait ninety seconds for that round of hormones to play out, then take a moment to ask myself questions like, "Is there any immediate danger to my well-being," or "Is it necessary for my safety to hold myself in this state of fear?" This was how I trained my own brain to calm down. It worked...for the most part.

At times, it seemed like the whole world was waiting to see what would finally bring me down. Even Leo kept telling me this time I would not fare so well. He was certain the trauma of your long illness and inevitable death would be the proverbial straw that broke the camel's back. My back.

It's such a strange thing to live with, that kind of judgment from others. It's an additional weight to carry alongside the grief. Why not encourage people like me instead? Why not tell me things like, "I can't imagine how you must be feeling, but I have faith you'll find healing." Or, "It must be very difficult to go through this, but just know you will survive." Or better yet, "I'm sure you must miss her terribly, but isn't it wonderful she offers you support and guidance from her new perspective beyond the veil?" Why can't these be our standard sentiments to the bereaved?

Instead, we tell others and ourselves there is no coming back from something like losing a child. If I occasionally had people tell me, "I don't know how you'll survive this. I know I couldn't do it," after your brother died, can you imagine how frequently I had to endure the "you poor dear" looks and ramped-up doomsday comments like, "It's just not fair! It's not right that you have to lose both your children. How are you still standing after such loss? How is it you can still function?"

By the time your cancer was diagnosed, I had learned a lot about how the brain works. Knowing the brain holds on to what we tell it to believe, I was able to deflect most of the comments folks innocently directed my way, believing they were shoring me up by telling me how much stronger than them I must be, when in reality, their comments required me to expend more precious energy to consciously direct my brain to believe something other than what they were telling me.

In other words, I had to pay attention. I had to focus on how their comment made me feel, and I often had to tweak, edit, or outright replace such statements with kinder versions inside my own head so my brain would not believe my life was a disaster I would never recover from. It was all very exhausting and unnecessary, really. If people only knew.

Other people weren't the only ones to complicate my grief journey, Dawtah. You, yourself, added a bit of an obstacle. I don't blame you for it—nope, not at all. It is one hit I willingly accepted and would volunteer to take again and again should you need me too. I know you'll remember doing it.

I'd use any tender moment between us as an opening to say things to you, things a mother would want her child to know before she left this world. I'd try to deliver sentiments of healing, love, and forgiveness so you'd float away to the afterlife on a cloud of love and comfort when your time finally came.

But no, you'd shut me down every time because it hurt you to cry, and you couldn't help but tear up during such intimate moments. I understood you meant it *hurt* you to cry. The tension and pressure in your head would override your pain meds as soon as a conversation got serious, and I could not bear causing you any more pain than you already had to endure, so I swallowed my own need to talk.

Even so, there was no way I was going to bury you without somehow healing our troubled relationship. If you couldn't openly talk about it, I would find other ways to show you how much I loved you. My solution was to create a palace for you in my home, where you would reside as a princess for your remaining time on earth. It was my gift to you, Dawtah, and it came at a heavy price, but one I would freely give to you over and over again if required.

Writing this brings all sorts of memories up like the day I brought a Shaman in to sit with you. She stayed for hours. Do you remember? Of course you do. She told us many things that helped us both come to terms with our journey together as mother and daughter, making sense of things we didn't understand about each other at the time.

I loved how that wise woman treated you with reverence, giving you the space and time you needed to take frequent cigarette breaks by the sliding doors in the dining room so you could watch your beloved birds come to the cluster of feeders Leo dutifully kept filled to their brims for you.

I rejoiced while watching you come to your own understanding of what your short life had been all about. I was able to breathe a sigh of relief to see you surrender control to your own Soul, finally trusting it to see you through whatever was to come.

And since I believed wholeheartedly in the theory of Soul Contracts, I was particularly touched to hear about my own place in the story of your chosen path for this life. It made perfect sense to me when the Shaman's otherworldly guides, who have access to all that is, ever was, and ever will be, told us a tale of how you chose to experience this most difficult path. They said having a mother who was a hard ass like me was required so I could be there for you through the treacherous road ahead, strong and sure-footed enough to see you through to the other side of it.

Her guides went on to explain all our earthly experiences are designed by us to teach us about love in all its many forms, and you had chosen this lifetime to experience the lack of love, explaining that to understand what love is, we first must learn what it isn't. The dawning of self-awareness that passed over your beautiful face in that moment will remain etched in my heart forever.

As I sat in the sacred space created for you in your room that day, I realized I was bearing witness to the moment you accepted the truth of it all. The life choices that led you to nothing but heartache and hardship were not mistakes after all, but a job well done as your own Soul had been guiding you the whole time through those painful learning opportunities.

Watching you release all judgment against yourself and relax into your fate was one of the most beautiful things I had ever seen. That, Dawtah, surely must be what they are referring to when they say someone "died with grace," because you certainly embodied the word that day.

I would later call upon that serene image of your face, using it like a healing balm to soothe my mind when it insisted on being fixated on visions of what you, my beloved daughter, had come to look like once the cancer finished wasting every part of your body. Because for me, that was the horror of it all. I was once again a mother who was powerless to do anything to stop her child's pain and suffering.

Watching my little girl waste away before my eyes was one of the hardest things I have ever had to endure. I found throughout it all, if my anxiety cranked up or my panic over the uncertainty of how and when your final breath would come started to rise, I could simply reset my train of thought by telling myself, "We still have time."

Yes, time was my biggest gift during your cancer journey because it's when I finally learned what living in the present moment was all about. And while most of my memories of caring for you those last nine months are a jumbled mix of long, task-filled days and short, mostly sleepless nights, there were also little pockets where time suddenly seem to stop, leaving just you and me floating gently somewhere between what was and what was yet to be.

I took my greatest pleasure and much comfort from those brief moments, flash-freezing them in my mind's eye to preserve them so I could call upon them in the future to sustain me when I needed propping up.

Those were the moments when our healing took place, Tierra. Those little snippets of "now" moments when we became focused on each other, like that day near the end when I brought you outside and sat you in a folding camp chair next to me while I replaced my fading summer annuals with chrysanthemums. I remember chattering away, explaining the whole process while you simply sat with your face tilted to the weakening early autumn sun.

I assumed you were not paying attention but off in your own world as I prattled on about giving the roots extra room and watering in the plant food before placing the new flower in the ground so as not to burn the tender shoots. But then you looked at me and said, "See? This is why I love you so much, Mom. Here I am getting ready to die, and you are still trying to teach me things. I just love it!"

If I close my eyes, I can still see us there. Mother and daughter, both at peace with each other and the world around us. My life has held few finer moments than that one, or this one right now as I dive deeper into the memory of it because it was one of many moments of surrender for me. I surrendered more fully to the process taking place within you—a process that was yours alone to endure but with a ripple effect traveling further than we could see at the time, affecting many people in ways we never could have imagined.

Choosing to cherish the time I had left with my daughter allowed me to fully relax into moments like the above, but to do so, I had to learn how to live in the present moment. I had to live in the "now" since the past no longer exists, and the future has not yet been written.

My foray into the world of Shamanism taught me the importance and relevance of using ritual and ceremony as a tool to help ease us into such a state of mind. When we set an intention to create a meaningful ritual or ceremony to mark a specific moment, we announce to ourselves and the world that something special is about to happen. We can feel an actual shift in the energy and a change in the posture of those in attendance. We know we've entered a poignant moment, a sacred space.

The ways you can create a ritual or ceremony to honor your deceased and focus on a now-moment made sacred is limited only by your imagination. Elaborate preparations and props are not necessary, but if they feel fun and/or appropriate at the time, by all means go all out. Here are a few simple suggestions for ways to bring ritual and ceremony into your daily routine.

Tips for Creating Ritual and Ceremony

1. **Set Your Intention:** Start by naming (out loud or on paper) your ritual's focus. For example, "To honor the deceased at holiday gatherings," or "To commemorate/celebrate the day they transitioned to the afterlife," or even, "To signify my willingness to let go of my pain."

2. **Decide Whom to Include/Invite:** Since you are the author of the ritual, you get to decide if you will keep it to yourself or share it with others. For example, you might want to keep a ritual created to connect to your

loved one in Spirit, focusing on receiving their forgiveness if you have unresolved relationship issues that are private to yourself. In a group, you can still share a ceremony to honor the day they passed into spirit each year.

3. **Prepare the Space Ahead of Time:** Ensure all preparations are completed before the assigned time for your ritual so your special time won't be cluttered with "busy work" and other distractions.

4. **Create a Sacred Space:** You can do this any number of ways. It doesn't have to be complicated. Play some soft, flowing music, and offer a simple prayer or a few spoken words to set the stage for those in attendance. Lighting a candle or, if it appeals to you, burning some sage, palo santos (holy wood), or incense would also shift the energy of the space to quiet reverence, showing those present something special is about to happen.

5. **Proclaim Your Intention:** State the intention you decided on ahead of time before you transition into the "moving parts" of your ritual or ceremony. If this is a simple candle-lighting ceremony, before you light the match, say out loud, "We wish to share this special occasion (birthday, holiday, anniversary, etc.) with our loved ones who have passed from this world. We light a candle for each of them to honor the lives they lived here on earth and welcome their presence at our table when the family gathers."

6. **Perform Your Ritual or Ceremony:** Perform the actions involved in your ceremony that you planned out ahead of time. Even the briefest moment, like lighting a single candle, can be a ritual if it is done with

intention and reverence. Say their names. "We welcome Adam, Tierra, and Leo. Come, join in our family celebration!"

7. **Create Closure to Your Ritual or Ceremony:** Once the ritual is completed, bring a sense of closure to your ceremony rather than ending it abruptly. This can be done by saying a second prayer, offering words of gratitude to those who participated, or encouraging folks to share a few thoughts about the person you are honoring before the group breaks up.

   Perhaps tell a funny story or two, something you remember about each person from past holidays like the Thanksgiving when deceased Uncle George dropped the turkey on the floor while taking it out of the oven or the time your late husband got caught encouraging your children to feed the dog their broccoli under the table at a Christmas dinner when they were little. This process fosters stronger feelings of connection, which bring peace to the soul of those who grieve and are just as important as the ceremony itself.

8. **Repeat as Often as Desired:** You can create as many rituals and hold them as often as you want without limits or restrictions. I believe both are artistic expressions of the Soul, so let's not put limitations on that. Some people live very "meditative lifestyles" by making a ritual out of everyday tasks like brewing and drinking their morning tea, moving through a sunrise yoga routine to greet the day, performing intentional breathwork, or writing in a journal before bedtime. Anoint yourself with a drop of your favorite essential oil and add a brief prayer or statement of intention before you start, and you've created a sacred ritual!

The type of activity you can make into a ritual really has no limits. Anything entered into with reverence and intention to honor or serve (yourself or others) can become ritualistic in nature simply by remaining focused on the beauty of your actions. I hope you try it. It really does help the mind shift from carrying grief as a heavy burden to experiencing it as a journey we are honored to be part of.

"Simply touching a difficult memory with some slight willingness to heal begins to soften the holding and tension around it."

— Stephen Levine

CHAPTER 7

SURRENDER: GIVING IN, NOT GIVING UP

Typically, we see two trains of thought when it comes to the word "surrender." Some view it as giving up when they feel they can't possibly go on or they believe they have no choice, leaving them feeling depleted and often ashamed they couldn't push past their struggle. They feel beaten and can easily become sullen, bitter, and even depressed, depending on how intensely the experience affects their lives.

I am of a second group who sees surrender in a more empowering way. When those like us say we have surrendered to an experience, it is simply our way of saying we vow to stop fighting what is happening and allow it to unfold in Divine timing. We trust ourselves, the Universe, or God to see us through. We evoke our faith that everything happens for a reason, and we relax into it. We give in and release the struggle, leading us to acceptance and leaving us feeling more peaceful and capable of handling what comes our way.

Which group do you find yourself in?

If you're having trouble divining the difference, you can easily check in with yourself to determine which is you. Just ask yourself how you *feel* about your decision to let go, stop fighting, and surrender. Do you feel ashamed or angry, as if you surrendered without really wanting to, giving up against your will, so to speak? Does it leave you feeling your life is out of control and you can do nothing to make things better? Do you feel you have *lost* the battle, whatever it is?

Or do you feel relief, less anxious, hopeful, or even empowered? Does it help remind you your own Soul is there to guide, assist, and even comfort you in times of great turmoil? Does it leave you feeling you have "someone" in your corner, willing to step in when the struggle is too much for you? In other words, do you feel "bad" or "good" about your decision to surrender?

The irony here is society demands we fight cancer with everything in our arsenal, yet it was the cancer itself that insisted I learn how to surrender. I had to stop fighting what was happening to my girl and find peace within myself so I could be a calming and soothing presence during her remaining days.

Even then, many more opportunities came where I had to consciously choose to stop fighting. Some came easily; others did not. Caring for the terminally ill in your own home is a highly stressful situation. It is physically, emotionally, spiritually, and yes, financially demanding. It puts enormous pressure on us, leaving us often short-tempered and emotional.

One fight during my daughter's illness I resisted releasing for a long time involved my son-in-law, Jerry's behavior. My irritation with him had begun long before we moved Tierra into my home for her end-of-life-care, but in those last few weeks of her life, I was able to peer inside his story and see his hidden fear and pain; as a result, I was able to change how I perceived his actions and surrender to his needs in all of this. Our power struggle was released the moment I made that shift, and life became much more peaceful for us all.

How easily we tend to judge another's actions is not lost on me, especially when we feel we are giving everything we have and they don't seem to be. We really can't know what is happening inside someone else's psyche. We don't know how easy or hard it is to be in their skin. We pass judgment based solely on how *we* think, feel, and process things. I was beginning to see the grief journey was packed with every life lesson you could ever need, all crammed into one intense experience that could not be ignored.

My ability to truly apply the art of surrender started the very day my daughter called to deliver the news of her diagnosis. While my body instinctively reacted with terror and panic at the thought of another child being ripped from my life, my mind immediately calmed when I realized we would have the gift of time on our side.

I remember elements of that call quite vividly. Not so much the words she was saying since I recall very little of the conversation past, "Mom, I have cancer," but the rapid-fire succession of thoughts and feelings passing through me left lasting impressions.

Denial came first as my mind refused to believe God would take both my children from me. My brain insisted it simply wasn't possible. Then I remembered a woman I used to work with who buried two of her three children, showing me it can and does happen.

Next came my natural tendency to remain positive, telling Tierra to hold on to hope and believe not all cancer diagnoses were death sentences, even though I had a sinking feeling hers would, indeed, take her life.

On the heels of that came all the questions, fast and furious, as I slipped into mother-caretaker role, gearing up for the hours of relentless research I would do in hopes of finding one sliver of information that would help my daughter beat the odds.

Then came the release. All my reactions played out one after another in a mere minute or two, finally resting on the realization we would have time. My own mind was showing me the way by reminding me to stay in the moment. Once those tumbling thoughts and emotions played out, I was able to relax into knowing we would have time to deal with all of this. We would face whatever was to come together, but that day, I still had a daughter with a live and beating heart, and she was on the other end of the phone looking for love and support. I did what any parent would do if they were able. I stepped up.

In this way, I found myself applying some of the principles I adopted while processing my grief over my son's death. I stayed in the moment, which helped relieve the anxiety threatening to overwhelm me because we didn't know for sure if she would live. And I practiced being truly grateful for the time we were given, which allowed us to use it to its fullest, healing our troubled mother-daughter relationship while we still could. I was doing it. I was working the program I hadn't yet realized I was creating!

(Dear Tierra, cont.)

I had "the dream" again last night. I hadn't had it nor thought of it for years. Not since a year or so after your brother was born. This time it took a bit of a twist. Back then when I had it, I always woke in a panic. A silent scream would be trapped in my throat that I had to swallow lest I wake the neighborhood. The background scene, set of circumstances, and the children themselves were different each time, but the theme of the experience was always the same.

In those dreams, I was playing out a typical mother's worst fear—having to choose one of her children over the other. Always some life-or-death drama was playing out like the one where the house is on fire, and I could only save one of you, or the nightmare about a plane crashing and exploding nearby, and I could only carry one of my toddlers while running through the debris to escape the fire. In those dreams, I always woke before making that dreadful choice, eternally frozen in panic and indecision.

The dream I just woke from was equally terrifying. I was standing on the bank of a muddy river, fraught with unseen dangers like alligators and such, when two children appeared nearby who were clearly not mine. The smaller one, whom I guessed was barely one since he was still walking with jerking motions, unsteady on his feet and unsure of his balance, fell into the churning river and immediately sank like a stone.

The second child, whom I assumed was his brother, was a bit older, maybe four or five. He jumped in after the first child, only to have the same thing happen. He was pulled down as if being towed under by an unseen hand.

I skipped only a fraction of a beat before jumping in myself. I quickly chose to go after the second boy since the first had already sunk out of view in the murky waters. But as is the way of dreams, the second boy was sinking ridiculously quickly, and I could not swim fast enough to catch up with him. I eventually had to decide to let them both go to their deaths to save myself.

I woke covered in a sheen of sweat, gasping for breath with, "I couldn't save either of them, but I could save myself," scrolling across my vision like a neon marquee announcing that evening's feature film. In that moment, I clearly saw that forces beyond my control, events you and your brother set into motion long before you emerged into this life from my own womb, had played out in the timing determined by your own Soul, and neither I nor anyone else could have done anything to stop it from happening.

What I also saw clearly is I did have my own choice all along. I could have given up and stayed in the muddy waters, forever searching for my lost children, refusing to give you up for dead, or I could swim to the surface toward the light and life-giving air.

I chose life. But to have that life, I had to let you go.

Today, I could recount all the little moments where, layer by layer, my resistance to your decided fate fell away. The first was the day you called from New York to announce that the lump you had removed from the side of your face was, indeed, cancerous.

At first, the resistance was there, loud and clear, as I passionately tried to assure you a cancer diagnosis these days did not necessarily mean death. But then I did what most mothers would do. I researched.

As I read the statistics about your carcinoma ex pleomorphic adenoma of the parotid gland, a.k.a. salivary gland cancer, my heart sank. (Can you believe I still remember that awful mouthful of foul-tasting words?) My thoughts turned stormy again.

"No! It's not possible. God simply wouldn't take my only surviving child away. Not like this!"

The research suggested a 50 percent survival rate if caught early enough (stages one or two). The size of your tumor, along with its multiple types of cancer cells, placed you at stage three.

When I went deeper, I clearly saw some reading between the lines was in order. The articles I found all seemed to agree that a 50 percent survival rate was indicated, but reading the fine print, I learned what that really meant.

It meant 50 percent of people with one of these malignant tumors will survive beyond the five-year mark. Those who live past five years only do so because their cancer is growing more slowly or spreading to areas of the body that do not immediately threaten life, but eventually, given enough time, they all succumb to the disease.

Your first oncologist later confirmed when he told us the story of a twenty-five-year-old woman who had come to his office some ten years prior with a similar tumor and outlook. He said she showed tiny spots in her lungs much like your films showed in those early days of your diagnosis and treatment. He said while scientists had not found a chemo cocktail that effectively treated your type of cancer, they were sometimes getting good results with aggressive radiation, which would hopefully slow everything down and, in some cases, even shrink tumors.

The problem, he said, was your tumor had grown all around the main nerve of your face. They couldn't remove it surgically without leaving microscopic bits behind. He explained how rare, invasive, and aggressive your cancer was. No treatment beyond surgery and radiation to slow things down existed.

The hope he offered was in the timing of your death. Perhaps the radiation would buy you enough time to watch your children grow up before the cancer took you. Perhaps.

But that was not to be your story, and part of me knew it then. I instinctively knew the cancer would take you to the grave sooner rather than later, but still, I chose to fight. I fought against the finality of it, convincing you to try all my vegan diet plans and carefully researched natural supplements to support a body riddled with disease and full of toxic chemicals.

I fought hard to believe my love along with months of superhuman efforts to keep your freezer stocked with organic, healthy foods; your apartment clean; and your kids entertained and cared for so you could live as stress-free as possible would ultimately save your life.

I tried to believe that, but somewhere deep inside, I heard little whispers of the truth. Your life was yours alone, and your own Soul was in charge, not me. The outcome was already decided.

When I learned one day after spending hours cooking meals for you and making the fifty-mile drive to your apartment to deliver them, that you sent Jerry out for Burger King and Snickers bars as soon as I left, I was confronted with the certainty that you did not want to fight this cancer.

I was confused and admittedly hurt when faced with this new truth—a truth I did not want to accept and immediately tried to explain away, choosing to see your actions as a temporary setback. I set out to prove deep down you really did want to live.

You readily agreed to a little experiment and easily participated as I guided you with softly spoken words into a state of deep relaxation. I purposely did not explain ahead of time what I intended to do during this experiment other than to give you instructions to respond with the first word that came to your mind when I made certain statements so you wouldn't be influenced in any way.

When ready, I spoke the first statement: "You have found a way to beat this cancer and will live a long, cancer-free life." Your immediate response was, "Panic."

I followed that with: "There is no stopping this cancer, and it will take your life within the next few months."

I felt the full weight of your single-word response, "Relief." You spoke it without hesitation and with a heartfelt sigh I simply could not ignore.

That was the day I stopped trying to help you (force you?) to live and began helping you to die. Making the shift itself flowed easily and naturally once I admitted to myself that it was what you wanted and released my own need to control the situation.

It was a pivotal point in our journey together and a big universal lesson for me. Today, I am most grateful for all of it. It was when I really found my faith—faith that my Soul was indeed in charge of my experience here on earth.

Because I had studied and come to believe such theories as Soul Contracts and our own sovereign nature as individual expressions of a Universal Consciousness (God), it became sort of what Oprah would call an "aha moment" for me.

In that decision to shift from a human mother instinctively keeping her child alive to a spiritual being who agreed to experience all this with you and stay by your side to help ease your journey, I donned a deeper, unshakable faith in the spiritual and metaphysical teachings I had adopted since your brother's death.

On that day, I began to genuinely walk the talk as they say. And that, Dawtah, was the second noticeable gift I was to receive from this experience…the gift of Faith.

Although I "got it" then and had no problem supporting you, my dying girl, in how you wished to live out your remaining days, I still fell into my old ego-driven, controlling behaviors with other people, especially those closest to the situation. But you weren't surprised by that, were you?

And so, I continued to fight. I fought against your husband, Jerry. At first because he didn't support my efforts to help you live, caving into your desires for the foods I saw as poisonous in your condition. But even after I made the shift to helping you die, I fought him.

Before Leo and I moved you into our house, I fought him over the state of your apartment and how he parented the kids while you tried to keep things together as a family for as long as possible. It infuriated me to find you lying in bed surrounded by dirty laundry and empty food containers, or worse yet, downstairs in your living room folding laundry when doing so obviously caused you excruciating pain. My pleas for him to step up and do more were met with blank, tight-lipped stares, so I would do what I could to tidy up, taking what dirty laundry I could carry home with me each week.

When you came to live your remaining days with Leo and me so you could keep the worst of your suffering from your children, I continued to fight him. I fought him when he came to visit on the weekends, spending every moment sitting with you, watching TV with you, chain-smoking outside with you, and even napping when you did, leaving me to care for your children. I'd give him lists of things that needed to be done around your room or the house in general, and he would nod and then leave on Sunday evenings without having done anything beyond visiting with you, leaving me frustrated and exhausted at the start of each work week while he went home well-fed and rested.

I fought him until Leo confronted him, accusing him of being lazy and selfish. Then I began to truly see your husband. Leo insisted he see how much I was struggling to keep everything together and pitch in to help. I was, after all, taking care of his sick wife seven days a week so we believed his visits should have served as a bit of a respite for me. I should have been able to enjoy the freedom to relax while he took over on the weekends.

But that was the story Leo and I were telling ourselves. Me because I felt I had no control of anything about the situation, and Leo because he also felt powerless watching his wife become drained and exhausted as the weeks of constant stress and work stretched into months.

Your husband had a different story. His story was one of a man who thought he had lost his family when his wife packed up the kids and left New York to move back to New Hampshire and start a new life without him. He couldn't see how badly she needed the support of her own family, her own mother, while she faced the uncertainty of living with a cancer diagnosis.

He had not given up. He had pursued his wife over the miles, eventually winning back his place in the family, only to learn the reunion would be temporary because death would soon separate him from his beautiful, young wife forever.

The man in that story was forced, against his will, to hand his beloved bride over to her mother once more when their small-town hospice team admitted they could no longer manage her complex symptoms and increasing pain levels, effectively shutting him out of the most important journey of her life. That man never understood why she wanted to leave their home during the most intense parts of her illness. He couldn't see past his own pain.

That man needed to spend every free moment with his wife. That man went home every Sunday night not knowing if it would be the last time he hugged his wife's warm body, lit a cigarette for her, or simply dozed next to her while she slept. That man was doing what he needed to do to survive his own story.

I'd love to say once I got it, once I had that brief glimpse inside his reality and felt Jerry's pain, I immediately became a more peaceful and loving person. But that's not what happened.

While I now recognize the experience as a life-changing epiphany, living it was far more difficult in the beginning. In fact, I still have to consciously work at it. I try, but I still sometimes react emotionally to another's behavior, triggering my human reaction to pass judgment.

But if I take a moment to consider another's motives, I can almost always recognize some kind of pain or fear hiding just behind the surface; that allows me to release my attachment to my view of that particular person or situation. It's liberating, actually, this "live and let live" attitude. I highly recommend it!

This process has a name: Surrender. Surrender was the third very noticeable gift I received during your illness.

Ironic, isn't it? While our culture encourages us to fight tooth and nail against cancer, the cancer taught me what it really means to surrender.

Religious people will see surrendering as giving their worry over to God. I simply choose a slightly different but equally effective way of seeing it. I believe that Higher Power to be my very own Soul. In this way, my mind understands I am not "giving my power away" to external circumstances. No, by surrendering, I am actually trusting my own Soul's purpose and allowing it to grab the wheel when I cannot make sense of where life is taking me. I trust my Soul will see me through.

It's easy to look back from where I sit today and see this situation all so clearly. But in the middle of the experience, too many distractions kept me from staying in a serene state for long. I simply couldn't sustain it at the time. I toggled between peace and struggle, surrender and fight, the duality of it not lost on me as I often seemed to be split between two worlds: the restrictive, drama-filled world of humans, and the ever-expanding world of Spirit.

I longed for you to find comfort in the same way, but you could not. Other than small pockets of time, like special visits from friends or the beautiful day you received Shamanic healing work, you could not find peace within your journey but lived with constant anxiety.

While most people assumed you were struggling against the finality of your situation, the real source of your angst was in the timing. You were anxious to be done with it. You just wanted to get it over with. Your perspective was different from mine. When it came to thoughts of the moment when death would come, you gave in to the overwhelming sense of dread and fear. You had surrendered in the "giving up" sense of the word, not in the more empowering way of trust and faith.

While I write about this, I hear you reminding me that the little peace you found along your treacherous and slippery slope came from being with me. Memories are flying through my mind of your face clearly relaxing when you saw me the first time each day and again when I returned from work each evening.

You told me so once. You told me my presence made you feel safe, and being with me was the best part of your day. Thank you for that, Tierra. Thank you for telling me that. It allowed me to see that while I, as your mother, could not take away your disease, I could still make you feel better just by being near. I could still mother you in that way.

But I cannot take all the credit for the moments of peace and comfort you experienced in those last months. I know in my heart it was a combined effort. The love you received from the constant stream of visitors bolstered you during the times I could not be with you myself.

You surprised me when you told me. We were in the car coming home from Plymouth after you had your central IV line placed. Watching you endure that procedure, I was overcome with sorrow for you, my daughter, and I told you so.

"I'm sorry, Tierra," I said. "I'm sorry you have to go through all of this." You didn't even hesitate. "Mom, don't you get it? I'm having the time of my life!"

I understood even more deeply then that this was, indeed, the path your own Soul had chosen for you. I knew you were not referring to all the suffering the physical illness brought but all the love and attention you got from family, friends, and community—something you had always felt starved for during this lifetime.

I still marvel at this, Dawtah. I know how hard it was for me to walk in grace when my discomfort overrode my peace, so I can only imagine how much effort it took for you to lay aside your horrendous suffering long enough to enjoy some precious moments with those who gifted you their time, all while knowing they were your last days on earth.

But that's just it, isn't it? It wasn't hard at all when you surrendered in the true sense of the word. It was easy. Easy to stay in each moment to savor the love, sipping it like a fine wine and letting it roll around on the pallet, delighting the senses before taking it into your belly. In those moments, you were the embodiment of peace and grace.

These are the memories I like to hold. Over the years, they have become more and more prominent in my mind as, one by one, they replace the heart-wrenching images of all the pain and suffering you endured in body, mind, and Spirit that threatened to dominate my thoughts during those early days of grief.

In this way, I have shaped my own grieving experience from one of never-ending anguish to a beautiful story of everlasting love that will be told in our family for generations. It's funny how simple it really is. Again, it comes down to perception. Our mind will believe anything we tell it, so I make it a practice to feed my mind beautiful truths, essentially starving out the damaging thoughts that try to take up long-term residence.

I began this practice after your brother's death, but I did not fully understand the concept until I walked this long, treacherous road with you, my girl. What I find so beautiful about life is how fluid and malleable it really is. Perception…another wonderful gift the cancer journey dropped at my feet. How can I not be grateful for it?

I really was a completely different woman at the time of your death than at the beginning of your illness. So much growth happened as each new awareness blossomed within me. But even so, the human experience had to be endured, demanding center stage the majority of the time.

Pulling your focus together long enough to make conscious efforts toward self-help and improvement is not always possible while in the middle of a trauma storm. Therefore, I believe it is beneficial to offer two avenues of hope for folks looking for grief support.

The newly bereaved and folks experiencing complicated grief symptoms are typically emotionally trapped within the experience (physically feeling the panic rise whenever their mind touches on the event—as if it had just happened), and deserve a safe place where their story can be tended to. They benefit most from having a place to gently explore their story in the company of others who are experiencing similar circumstances. They need a place where they are encouraged to express all the feelings that come up, no matter how *crazy* or *wrong* they mistakenly believe them to be. They need a place where fear can take a backseat as they begin to understand the dynamics of their grief and how it will move through them once they learn how to allow it. They need a place where they are thrown a life preserver in the form of a community of folks teaching by example that hope is within reach before asking them to move on to what I consider "PT" (Phase two—

the physical therapy of grief support). There they are asked to willingly experience their pain with the intention of learning what it has to teach them and accepting the gifts it offers.

Since I did not have such a place to go to after Adam died, I spent my time intentionally observing my own patterns of behavior and emotional responses in hopes of finding the "magic key" that would release me from the chains of grief. I also continued to search *outside myself* for healing, bouncing from holistic practitioners for hypnosis sessions and reiki treatments, to psychic mediums for Soulful connections and Shamans for ritual and ceremony. If you recall, I did eventually find a therapist I checked in with from time to time during that first year or so after Adam's suicide.

While I certainly hadn't learned everything I needed to know about processing grief in healthy ways in that first profound experience of sudden loss, all of the efforts described above served to open my mind to the possibility of achieving peace *while living with grief.* As it turns out, that was all I needed to patch me up and prepare me to face the challenge before me, which was to walk my daughter to death's door without losing my mind.

When I opened this part of my journey, where my only remaining child delivered the dreaded news of her cancer diagnosis, you saw how I immediately reached for the not-yet-broken-in tools I had discovered since Adam's passing and began wielding them whenever I could during this arduous chapter in my story of transformation through loss. Let's take a look at how that went for me as the stress of caring for someone so critically ill intensified. Do you think I was able to sustain my positive attitude throughout?

*"I am more vulnerable
than I thought,
but much stronger than
I ever imagined."*

— Sheryl Sandberg

CHAPTER 8

TWO BIRDS, ONE STONE

Worldwide, people have shared stories of communicating with the afterlife since civilization began. You'll remember how I was introduced to the healing power of experiencing a deceased loved one's presence after my son died. My daughter Tierra, from beyond the grave, taught me how we could actually interact with one another. I learned to lean on her in many ways, and when I ask for help, she is always there to facilitate just what I need, when I need it.

Being so intimately involved in caring for someone close to you who is expected to die is one of life's richest experiences, if you choose to view it that way. The journey is ripe with opportunities to learn, heal, and grow. Tierra's illness took two years to run its course, leaving me lots of time to think and ponder big questions like, "What are we here for? What is the purpose of this life?"

During the last few months of Tierra's illness, when I cared for her full time in the home I shared with my husband Leo, I really began to dig deeper into my own life story, realizing I could benefit from applying some of what I had been learning about grief to my life in general.

At that time, I was also dealing with a failing marriage that involved a difficult struggle with codependency, something often seen in relationships where alcoholism and emotional disturbances abound. I'll show you more of what it was like to live with the stresses involved in that situation when I get to Leo's story. I only touch on this now as a segue into the following account of contact with my deceased daughter, which involved planning a memorial service for Leo after his suicide in the summer of 2012.

Notably, while I struggled with reining in my complex feelings around Leo's suicide, Tierra—in her bodiless state of light and love—helped me relax and open my heart so I could get in touch with the part of me that had always loved my husband regardless of the issues he fought to control during our ten-year relationship. It is commonly believed among those who embrace the existence of the afterlife that once we leave our body, we also leave our ego-mind and human emotions behind, so I understood Leo now existed in a state of pure loving energy and could no longer hurt me.

What does that mean exactly? Well, to sum it up, when we die, we are no longer concerned with earthly matters. We leave behind all those human aspects that kept us grounded to this physical world such as worry, judgment, and fear. We no longer live with a fight-or-flight mentality, and we are able to see the bigger picture of what this human experience is here to teach us.

Therefore, our interactions with loved ones on the other side always come from a place of peace, understanding, and love. These out-of-body attributes extend to all of humanity, regardless of age, race, religious belief or lifestyle. As light-beings, devoid of human ego and emotion, they clearly see and understand the importance of having both light and dark, good and bad, love and fear in our daily lives because within the construct of these contrasts, we humans are offered opportunities to choose for ourselves what is right. How would we know we prefer light if we've never experienced the dark?

This next portion of my letter to Tierra showcases how that duality showed up frequently while caring for my daughter. It seems I was constantly being presented with opportunities to choose for myself how my story would play out. Again and again, with a little conscious effort, I could alter how I experienced something others saw as painful, renaming the experience as an honor rather than a burden, choosing to feel grateful instead of victimized. But would I be able to put this newfound gift of perception-control into practice when presented with Tierra's death scene? Would I face it with the reverence and sacredness the moment deserved, or collapse into despair, my own discomfort causing me to miss out on the intimacy of the experience?

(Dear Tierra cont.)

Nine months you lived while dying in my home. I find it strangely fascinating how that corresponds to the gestation period for the human embryo before it is born into this world. Nine months to bring you into this world, and nine months to escort you out, for it truly was a parallel journey to the birthing experience.

And much like giving birth to a living child is intensely painful but gloriously satisfying, walking you to the threshold of the afterlife was extremely challenging but also a very sacred and gratifying experience. After all, how many parents do you know who can say they were able to do this? That they were there to see their child take their first breath as well as their last?

Seeing things in this way allowed me to be grateful for all of it. I saw the holiness of it and the great honor in it. I chose to view it that way, for I could have just as easily chosen to carry it like a burden for the rest of my life, believing the fates had visited something upon me that there was no recovering from.

I added this perspective to the list of proof I was presenting to my own brain that I did have options when it came to my thoughts and feelings, and by choosing more empowering thoughts, my experience would be much lighter and easier to pass through. To struggle against it would have brought more obstacles and discomfort. This I know to be true.

I am so very grateful to myself for doing that inner discovery work because it allowed me to be fully present with you during the time it took you to wriggle your way out of your disease-ridden body. I was able to focus on what was happening to your Soul as it finally broke free from the confines of its cancer-riddled prison, and rejoice in the moment I sensed you standing in the corner of the room with your brother, watching your empty body struggle for the life-sustaining breath that would not come.

A duality existed in that scene. The part of me that was your mother threatened to override the reverence of the experience with rising panic at the sight of her child choking and gasping for breath with lungs that had quit working altogether, your body finally giving up and sinking into the mattress while your mouth worked with barely perceptible efforts to pull in air, resembling a tiny bird searching blindly for sustenance from its parents in the nest.

That image of you, looking like a dying baby bird, stayed with me and haunted my dreams both at night and during my waking hours for a long time to come. Not until I asked for your assistance in writing the eulogy I would deliver at Leo's memorial service did you help release me from the grip of that horrifying memory.

In keeping with your true personality, which included a markedly warped sense of humor, you literally used a dying bird to break the spell that particular vision had over me. I will never forget it because it brought great relief and joy-filled laughter during another terribly difficult time of my life, and I can't thank you enough for being there when I needed you.

Just shy of two years after your death, Leo took his own life, leaving me in a state of confusion and conflicting emotions. We naturally want to put our dead on a pedestal, yet Leo was staying close, reminding me not to forget the ugly truths of his own disease of alcoholism and abusive behaviors that intimately affected me during our years together.

On many levels, I could see the value in what he showed me, whispering "Don't forget, Vic" in my mind and showing me stark images of his face when it was contorted with rage, but that made it very difficult for me to write the loving, heartfelt words that everyone needed to hear on the day we gathered to celebrate all that was good about him and his life.

I called out to you just a couple of days before his life celebration to help me write what needed to be said. You were always so poetic when you put your thoughts on paper, and I knew you would not disappoint your mom.

After turning the worry of writing over to you before bed, I slept the first dreamless night in many. The next morning, I awoke anxious to get started, and while the house was still quiet in the early dawn hours, I set about preparing a comfortable workspace.

After taking the dogs out and fixing a strong cup of tea, I rounded the corner to my bedroom just in time to see a small bird fly directly into the sliding glass doors that led to the deck outside. That bird fell to the floor of the deck and lay with its feet up. Its little beak opened and closed with its last gasps for breath before expiring while I stood dumbfounded, watching.

Anyone else in this situation might have allowed that incident to send them right over the edge into a blubbering mass of tears, but I immediately recognized it as your way of killing two birds with one stone (pun most definitely intended!). It showed me you were, indeed, there to support my efforts to write something meaningful for Leo, and also to, once and for all, dispel that horrifying image of you as a fragile dying bird that my mind had refused to let go of.

It worked, Tierra. I could barely control my laughter, I couldn't wait until the others in the house woke so I could relay the story, and I never fixated on that terrible image again. Thank you, my girl. Thank you.

While we're on the subject of Leo, I want you to know how grateful I am to you for all the patience you offered him during your hospice days in our home. While his mood swings and quick-to-fire temper were causing me great distress, you would remind me he was just having trouble dealing with all the new people coming and going at our little hideaway in the woods. You showed compassion for him at a time when I could not, and I am most grateful for that.

In the end, I was glad he happened to be home the day you finally let go of this earthly life. He later admitted to me that up until then he hadn't quite believed you were dying; instead, he had held resentment because he thought you were playing me to get attention.

Until then, I couldn't comprehend how he could be so cruel to both you and me during the months you were with us, but this admission helped me understand his actions and behavior were a direct result of how he perceived the situation. He truly believed the lie he was telling his brain, the one where you made the whole thing up just to get attention.

This was a pivotal lesson for me about our ability to convince our minds of certain truths *and* lies. If he could watch nurses come day after day to increase your pain meds while your body was obviously being ravaged by disease, yet still somehow believe you were faking it, wouldn't it stand to reason we could train our minds to believe other, more uplifting truths?

I grabbed that concept and ran with it. Interestingly enough, it turned out I had been intuitively applying it since I was faced with your brother's death and chose to believe I could survive the grief rather than damning myself to a life of unbearable pain as scripted.

The busy work of caring for your physical needs while simultaneously attending to my spiritual and emotional ones left me lacking when it came to caring for my health. If I could go back and do anything differently, it would be to take better care of my body. While my mind and Spirit grew stronger through my grieving experiences, my body grew weaker and sicker as I buried whatever I could not process in the very tissues, bones, and organs trying to support my physical life.

You see, I was telling lies to my mind like, "It's okay to eat comfort foods and things like chocolate because they make me feel better," or "I can worry about this later. Right now I need to power through," or "I'll just swallow this emotion now so I can stay strong for T and her kids." On and on the lies flowed into my mind where they took up residence until such a time as they could no longer be ignored.

Now, in my sixties, I am finally addressing the body, for those buried feelings have spread and grown to a point where they can no longer be kept hidden. They are now clamoring to be seen, heard, and released for healing. I still have much work to do.

Realizing this, it all became clear how appropriate it was for me to move to Florida when I did. Being so far from everyone gave me the space and time I needed to concentrate on my remaining inner healing, and access to fresh air and outdoor activities year-round has helped me maintain a positive attitude while going through some pretty intense physical challenges in the four years since I arrived.

It's also fascinating that every time I make a healthy lifestyle change, a period of emotional release immediately seems to follow. This became quite evident earlier this summer when I watched from afar your youngest graduate from high school.

I almost missed it. With my laptop in the shop, I tried to watch on my cheap little tablet, but the video stream would not play. I assumed there was a problem with the website or a technical issue at her school, so I gave up trying to load it after thirty minutes or so.

Did you see me dissolve into a puddle of tears when I realized I would miss it? For reasons still unknown to me, I become overly emotional over the silliest things. This happens more and more lately, and I've been wondering why. Even after a couple of decades of consciously working on myself from within, why would I suddenly become so weepy?

Then it hit me. My newfound ability to cry at the drop of a hat is the healing! I see now how important this ability is for me since I had previously swallowed my tears to avoid hurting you. You see, Dawtah, I had pushed them back so often it became second nature, eventually making it difficult for me to cry altogether.

Imagine my surprise when, after drying my tears, a little voice I recognized as yours whispered in my ear, suggesting I try to watch on my phone. As you know, I don't always heed that voice, but I did in that moment and was just in time to watch Qwynn walk to the podium for her well-deserved diploma. The joy I experienced then was huge, especially as it came directly on the heels of such an emotional release.

I'm not surprised many of the contacts I receive from you involve family happenings, especially when those events include your children somehow, illustrating how family ties and connections are still important to you. I'm also tickled to see you using Raccoon whenever possible to help us make those connections.

I'll never forget the look on your face the night I did that Shamanic journey with the intention of bringing back an animal's "essence" to act as liaison between you, once you were back in the Spirit realm, and those of us still here on the earthly plane. We made a pact that you would seek ways to use raccoons as a symbol of your presence so we would recognize unusual sightings of said animal as a clear sign you were there with us.

You, like most others who experience this for the first time, were hoping for a sleek and impressive animal like a black panther or a lynx, so when I announced, "Raccoon has volunteered!" you could not hide your obvious disappointment.

But once I read you Raccoon's attributes, its creative nature and ability to adapt to any situation, a harbinger of change and transformation, your interest was piqued. Together, we went on to learn Raccoon was indeed a wonderful spirit animal to have on your side because it often served as guardian and protector to those it loves, which spoke directly to your own heart's desire to continue offering such services to your young children after your death.

Add to that the well-known reputation Raccoon has for being a "trickster," which mirrored your own mischievous personality, and it became pretty clear you received the perfect animal to act as your spirit guide after all. I love how quickly and easily you seemed to command those nocturnal creatures to do your bidding (or were you manipulating us so we'd stumble upon various sightings at "just the right time"), the first magical encounter coming just one week after your death.

My studies into the afterlife have trained me to recognize signs from the deceased by noticing the context in which they occur. In other words, sometimes a penny is just a penny, but finding a penny inside the shoe you just picked up to put on while having a particularly difficult time missing your deceased loved one on their birthday most surely is a "penny from heaven," a sign you are seen and supported in your suffering.

Even so, I still found ways to challenge and doubt certain contacts, explaining them away using common earthly circumstances. But having a mother raccoon walk across the road in front of my car with, "coincidentally," three little ones happily trailing behind her in broad daylight was a sign that could not be explained away rationally since raccoons are nocturnal creatures by nature and typically have their young in the spring…not late October.

I was driving to work on a Friday morning, thinking about the weekend when I would have my grandkids to myself for the first time since your death. I was planning the things we would do to honor your memory and encourage your kids to learn to sense you around them. I remember thinking how important it was to make sure they understood they still had your love and support while they were growing up, even though you could not tie their shoelaces and wash their little faces anymore.

The three of them listened raptly as I recounted the story of the Mamma Raccoon and her three little kits. That weekend, they all started collecting "special pennies" when they miraculously showed up in strange places and meaningful ways.

While these activities and stories helped foster their connection to their mamma in Spirit, I knew from my research and intuition as they grew and entered different stages of development that they would each face fresh bouts of grief over losing you so young.

Surely, times would come in each of their lives when they would wish they could see their mom in the audience when they received their high school diploma or take you for a drive when they got their driver's license, and of course, placing your first-born grandchild in your arms shortly after bringing them into the world.

I know you appreciate my efforts to keep your memory alive in the family and especially in the hearts of your children, the youngest of whom is struggling with "lost memories" of you. She was too little when you died to have developed more permanent impressions. Luckily, we took the time while you were still with us to capture lots of photographs and video clips and create little keepsakes to leave them something of you to cherish.

I love how "death doulas" are gaining more popularity these days in our culture since I've seen first-hand how helpful it can be for all involved to restore a sense of sacredness to the dying process. Engaging the whole family in actively caring for the dying not only helps ease their anxiety but gives the rest of us a sense of purpose in an otherwise hopeless situation.

I also love how willing you were while you still had breath left in you to participate in our plans for ritual, ceremony, and eventually, memorial services for you. It helped us all feel closer to you at a time when you were pulling back from the living, preparing to leave this world, and already looking toward the next. One foot in and one foot out, as it were.

You sat majestically, almost queen-like, the day we put you in a chair on the spot where we would place your memory stone and plant your favorite lilacs once you were gone. You seemed to soak it all up as we encircled you and placed our hands on your head, shoulders, and arms. Your kids and closest family all poured out loving energy into your warm, physical form while we still could, cementing a connection between those present and that particular plot of hallowed ground.

You listened carefully while we talked about plans to involve the children in a candle lighting ceremony during your memorial service so they would feel included in the send-off we were to give you, often suggesting edits or making sure to instruct us to watch the littlest of your littles closely around the flaming candles, forever the doting mother.

By doing this, we all felt strongly bonded, so after your death, it was a very natural step for us to adapt the same candle-lighting ceremony to important family meals like Thanksgiving, Christmas, and Easter, effectively ensuring a seat at the table for you as we gathered to celebrate life in all the ways families do.

I no longer have the large property in the woods to host big family gatherings, but still, the bag containing all the candle-lighting supplies hangs in my bedroom closet no matter where I live, patiently waiting for an occasion to make an appearance.

It's funny how a seemingly simple thing like lighting a candle for you at the family dinner table and speaking your name has an immediate and palpable effect, charging the room with quiet yet uplifting, loving energy, and leaving us all understanding we have somehow entered a "sacred space."

This is why I encourage people in grief to find and engage in various ceremonies of their own. The practice really does help shift one's perception of grief from a burdensome suffering to a more sacred task where we feel truly honored to have had our loved ones in our lives, even for such a short time. In this way, we are gently guided into a state of acceptance, something absolutely necessary if any real healing is to take place within us while we grieve.

Do you sometimes hear a voice inside your head, which seems to be you, or maybe "another version of you," that often comes in the form of a little whisper (although sometimes a big shout is more like it!) lovingly suggesting you steer your attention or your actions in a different direction?

Some call this their conscience or intuition. Others feel an angel or even God is offering this guidance. As far as I'm concerned, it doesn't really matter where that "voice" is coming from. Simply acknowledging its existence is the most important step in recognizing we are, indeed, receiving some type of guidance that seems to be "separate from" or "different from" our normal, daily, more dominant train of thought.

Once we make this observation, it is only human to become curious about the phenomenon, so some of us begin to seek deeper understanding while others are content to just take it's advice or not, depending on how they are feeling about their circumstances at the time.

How about you? Do you listen to that little voice in your head, or do you shush it when it seems to want to pull you too far out of your comfort zone?

I have learned to listen. While I don't always heed its advice, I do at least consciously listen. When I do follow its lead, I am always rewarded with some takeaway like a kinder, gentler path through whatever I am dealing with at the time. Likewise, if I deny what it asks of me and take my dominant, ego mind's choice of action, I more-often-than-not come away thinking, *I should have listened.*

I personally believe that inner voice of reason is my own Higher Self or Oversoul, the part of me that embodies perpetual grace, the keeper of the very spark of life that animates my human form. I also recognize this other aspect of me is responsible for guiding me throughout my life (or *lives* if you believe in reincarnation…same Soul, multiple lives).

Because of its eternal nature and infinite stature, I wholeheartedly believe that *It* (which is really *Me!*) has the ability to communicate and interact with the Souls of my departed loved ones and any other benevolent beings who may exist outside our normal earthly experience and human awareness. In this way, I am able to enjoy the "essence" of my deceased children as they make themselves known to me through various signs and synchronistic events.

Tapping into this unseen world around me excited me beyond anything I had ever encountered up to that point. When the world around me, which I always thought of as solid and predictable, proved to be nothing but an illusion that could be blown to bits after one child's decision to die, I could always find solace and comfort by simply connecting to this Spirit World through methods like meditation, journaling, lucid dreaming, or consulting with a psychic medium.

Each encounter with my deceased children served not only to comfort and support me, but it helped open my mind and strengthen my faith in the process I was going through. One by one, I began to practice more conscious living methods, which not only honed my ability to "hear" my kids, but led me to discover and weed out various beliefs and behavior patterns within myself that were not conducive to a healthy life. I was learning to live more fully and authentically.

Let's dive a bit deeper into the type of self-discovery my grief journey and resulting exploration into the world of Spirit led me to. Keep in mind the grief itself was visited upon me, so to speak; I didn't really have a choice in how and when my children left this world, but I did have many choices to make each and every day after their deaths. I kept choosing to work on it. I kept choosing to ask the questions and hunt down the answers. I kept choosing to *allow* the grief to change me. I kept choosing to grow from it.

What will you choose for yourself today?

"Never. We never lose our loved ones. They accompany us; they don't disappear from our lives. We are merely in different rooms."

— Paulo Coelho

CHAPTER 9

DIGGING UP BONES

While my experience with my son Adam taught me how to survive the devastating loss of a child, my journey with Tierra opened a door to further explore the nature of the Soul and the unseen world around us. This prompted some deep inner work, which led to discovering and unveiling my "shadow-self" and learning to accept and love her.

Before I could enjoy the spoils and riches this enlightenment brought, I had to endure the grueling process of excavating all the old conditioning and behavior patterns I had adopted along the way. I call this process "digging up bones" because, much like the elephant we find standing in the room deserves to be acknowledged, the skeletons in our closets also need to be brought out into the light of day if we want to live an authentic life, true to who we really are.

We can try cutting these parts out, but they will only grow stronger as they fight for survival, demanding their rightful place, showing up in our lives much like a malignant cancer sneaks around unseen until it has spread throughout the body, endangering our life.

Hiding secrets from others is one thing, but we tend to try to hide the shadow-self even from ourselves. We have all lost our composure enough to act out emotionally at times, saying and even doing things we immediately regret but cannot take back. Our culture thrives on order, so we are taught to be reasonable and control ourselves. We are shown losing control is shameful. And so, we hide.

Previously, we talked about how my foray into the world of metaphysics and my experiments with conscious-living methods like meditation and Shamanic journeying brought me peace and a certain measure of acceptance after Adam's suicide. You witnessed how these efforts birthed the curiosity within to discover a deeper understanding of the human experience. These insights helped me surrender to life's biggest challenges like caring for my dying daughter.

You watched as I shared some of what I learned with Tierra as she struggled with her illness and looming death, helping her accept her fate as much as possible given the circumstances. You've felt the love that can surface in the face of such tragedy and seen the healing it can bring to a family when they work together, intent on honoring the passing of one of their own.

While all this was extremely important in illustrating how you too can find a healing path after such tragedy, I consider sharing my shadow-self icing on the cake.

The following is an unexpected experience that came to me only now, in my sixties, more than a decade since Tierra died. I find it perfectly appropriate to close my letter to her with this account. With the bravery her eldest child has shown in coming forward, we have fulfilled the wise old Shaman's prophecy, bringing a damaging deep generational behavior pattern in our family to light to be healed. We've done it, Skyla and me. We've come full circle and given Tierra's life and death more purpose and meaning by healing this collective, generational wound.

(Dear Tierra cont.)

Being on a conscious path of self-exploration for the purpose of healing does not mean I am joyful all the time. The process of self-discovery can actually be extremely difficult and painful as I dig into the deepest, darkest reaches of my psyche to discover, confront, and shed light on those parts of me referred to as the "shadow-self."

While you and I did much to heal our mother-daughter relationship before you died, we left one big elephant in the room, never formally addressing it before you left—my darkest shadow-self, the one I've spent a lifetime hiding from. It is the self who takes over and turns me into someone I do not recognize, someone I cannot love. It is the one who, when freed from the deepest parts of my being where it sleeps, waiting its chance to emerge, expresses itself passionately with one goal in mind—destruction—and its name is *Rage.*

No one likes to admit they have a dark side. Especially those of us deemed "lightworkers." We can't admit to the world we are not made solely and completely of sunshine and daisies. We do not want the world to know we experience fits of anger, anxiety, and depression just like everyone else at one time or another. All the things society abhors are kept locked away lest we be discovered for who we truly are, a complex being with both light and dark forces residing within us.

When I take a moment to imagine a world where we trust each other, where we feel safe enough to show all our faces to each other without fear of judgment and ostracization, I can clearly see how lovely that world would be. Because, as you know from personal experience, to deny a big feeling like rage, to stuff it down and keep it hidden without allowing it to express itself, only creates a pressure cooker environment where it will thrive and grow to epic proportions while it bides its time waiting for sweet release.

If, instead, we could practice compassion for one another, and especially for ourselves, perhaps we would all learn to express our needs, wants, hurts, and desires when they arise and with more kindness and authenticity rather than passing judgment on them. Perhaps then we could all live in harmony.

Any of these things we leave unsaid, hidden away in captivity within our subconscious, will fester, just like your cancer, eating us from the inside out without our knowledge until the day comes when something happens to weaken our defenses, allowing it to break free from its chains, ready to unleash its anger on the world.

So here we are, Dawtah, finally talking about this openly and with painful honesty, you and me. And since I know you are aware of how the lives of your loved ones are unfolding here on the earthly plane, you must have watched with great pride as your firstborn did the most difficult thing by calling this shadow-self of mine out of hiding with a genuine desire to know and understand it.

It makes so much sense to me now that I have had a few days of complete solitude to sit with these memories and the feelings they brought up. I was horrified to see myself through your child's eyes. The child born to you as your own daughter Skyla. According to the Shaman's Guides, you had stepped in to fill the role of mother to her since I was "not ready to guide her" as my own during my childbearing years.

I had to feel the gut-wrenching pain as I stood naked and exposed before a mirror watching the various dramas of the past play out while fighting my own desire to stuff them all back into their respective storage bins, keeping them forever locked away in the darkest recesses of my mind. I pulled them up and out with the driven purpose of owning, understanding, and eventually releasing them with love, these things I had never acknowledged were part of me.

One by one, the memories came like scenes from a movie, complete with surround sound and over-the-top theatrics. I saw that other version of myself rush forward when my patience snapped over some form of parental defiance seemingly so inconsequential that now I cannot even remember what it was.

I saw my own face, contorted with rage as if seen from your adolescent eyes, as I screamed horrible and insulting words at you while in the throes of this thing I could not control, and I watched with bone-crushing shame as the young mother I was told her teenaged daughter she cannot wait until she turns eighteen so she can throw her out of the house.

The process brought me to my knees as I accepted that, yes, I really did do those things. And because the beast called Rage hadn't satisfied its hunger, it destroyed your sense of self-worth. This showed up again when Skyla was about the same age as you had been, with me visiting the same atrocity on her. The scenario was different, as were the ugly words spewed from Rage's/my mouth, but still, its goal was realized and the result was the same. The child began to believe she was unwanted and unlovable.

This is what your eldest brought to my door recently. This is what Skyla dug up out of her own psyche all by herself after experiencing a surprising and painful relationship breakup. She recognized a "theme" unfolding in her life, and she went digging for the origins with a desire to learn from it so it doesn't have to keep repeating.

By doing so, your firstborn has broken a behavior pattern generations deep. Similar behavior could be found in you, me, my mother, and hers before her. For me, this dawning of awareness was like waiting for the sun to rise. I had to sit completely alone in utter darkness with it as feelings of shame, guilt, denial, acceptance, fear, self-loathing, forgiveness, and grief all tumbled about while "the watcher" in myself understood the whole time that the sun would indeed rise, bringing with it the beautiful golden glow and glimmer of hope only a new day can offer.

With that first sunrise came my ability to see clearly through the veil, while still sitting with my human emotions. I could see it all from a Soul Contract or spiritual perspective:

If what the Shaman's Guides said was true, and you were meant to be a stand-in for Skyla, a placeholder until I was ready to give her the experience she contracted for in this lifetime, then it all makes perfect sense to me because she seemed to be picking up "our story" right where you and I had left off.

The similarities are so obvious to me now because Skyla seems to be repeating your journey of struggle by choosing friendships and partnerships that allow her to play the role of the unloved and abandoned.

But she did something different by speaking up with a heartfelt intention to heal, while you and I simply went head-to-head in a constant power struggle that never led to a resolution. Obviously, I "wasn't ready" to process this pattern of behavior with love and kindness at that time. I would have been crushed under the weight of self-loathing, much like I believe Leo was when he took a long look in the mirror, coming face-to-face with his own demons the day he decided to leave this world behind.

I did not know who that woman was when she was taken over by that kind of rage, and my judgment of her resulted in simply denying her existence altogether. I've denied my responsibility for her, essentially abandoning her too.

As awareness of this washed over me, I could see the relevance of my relationship with Leo in a new light. For now, I can see we were the same, he and I. We had childhood wounds that, when left unaddressed, had no choice but to show up in our adult lives as aggressive behavior. It's pretty widely known the "bully" originally becomes a bully to hide their fears and insecurities, making them feel like they are in control of their life.

I can see Leo and his role in my life more clearly now. I can see how damaged he was as a hurt little boy in a big, strong man's body. I can see the mirror he offers me now, and as painful as it is, I must take a good, long look. I mustn't turn away from what I see.

I wish you and I could have done this thing together while you were still here. But our time together as mother and daughter was spent in so much frustration. I was ill-equipped to teach you anything beyond what we found in books or watched on TV. I hadn't been introduced to the unseen world around us and the vast resources it holds until your brother's death. I suppose this is what that wise old Shaman meant when she said you had volunteered to reserve the role of my daughter for Skyla, "the one who would usher in change," until I was ready to play my part in the whole thing.

By confronting me in the compassionate and genuine way she did, Skyla instantly changed the outcome of it all. I am "ready" to hear it now, to look at it, to own it. Together, we can learn to understand this thing that doesn't even feel like it belongs to me—it is a complete 180 from what my mind and heart truly think and feel most of the time.

So, here I am counting shadow work as yet another blessing bestowed on me after your death, a gift I might never have received had I lived through a different set of circumstances. And if Adam's death sparked my interest in spirituality and yours fostered a deeper understanding of the Soul's journey here on earth, then Leo's sudden and dramatic death by suicide served to crack me wide open in ways I couldn't even imagine at the time.

Still, Dawtah, it seems you paid a very high price for these potent and wonderful gifts. I can't help but find myself toggling between quiet reverence with a huge sense of gratitude and a horrifying sense of guilt over not being worthy of such wonderful discoveries and all the perks that come with them.

But there you are assuring me, guiding me, directing me, and supporting me when I stumble. In you I feel like I have a mother, friend, cheerleader, and teacher, all wrapped up in a dreamy, ethereal package of angelic stature—until you wield your morbid sense of humor in your frequent contacts by showing me dead birds or raccoons with perfect timing. During those moments, I see your signature "devilish" grin, the one you wore regularly on your beautiful face. It was the look that made you into you in this lifetime. Those are the experiences I hold most dear today. Thank you, Dawtah. Thank you for choosing me to be your mom and for entrusting me with your first-born. I am forever humbled and grateful.

So how did I do? Can you see how I "practiced what I preached" and applied more and more of what I was learning to this episode of grief and loss? Do you see and understand the concept of "finding the gifts in grief" that people like me talk about? And can you see a change within me, making me a much different woman than the one you met at the beginning of this book who had just lost her eighteen-year-old son to suicide on Mother's Day?

In exchange for taking a life, a terminal cancer diagnosis will offer you the gift of *time.* And providing hospice care for my dying daughter, even though it was taxing for me on so many levels, set the stage for long hours of self-reflection where I could find and latch onto other "gifts" being presented to me, like gaining a broader understanding of the power of *surrender* and my deepening sense of *faith* in myself to see me through.

You watched me as I first learned how to apply "conscious living" methods (which simply means I am paying attention to what is happening within and intentionally applying various methods to improve anything I am not happy with) during my grief journey after Adam died. And you have witnessed how effectively things like *focusing on the now* dropped treasures at my feet I will cherish forever, like the memory of my daughter sharing those most precious words of love and gratitude with me while I planted autumn flowers in my gardens.

Perception, of course, is the big one, the big takeaway from all of this because once we understand our own perception of a circumstance either holds us in a pattern of anger, pain, and hopelessness, or sets us free to enjoy a more peaceful countenance, we have the proper tool to change how we experience anything that comes our way going forward. Change your perception and your whole life changes.

Do you still doubt? Are you having trouble believing you, too, can achieve this attitude? Go ahead; try it out. Pick something simple to start with, something you are not emotionally invested in like the woman in front of you at the pharmacy who has a million questions before the line can move forward, or the accident causing you to be stuck in a traffic jam, putting you behind schedule. The next time something like this irritates you, make a *conscious effort* to try to shift your perception.

As soon as you *decide* to try it, the shift begins to happen. Next, pay attention to what you are feeling about this disruption. Is it anger? Frustration? Worry you are going to be late? Where is it showing up in your body? Is your jaw tense? Your brow furrowed? Fists clenched? Stomach queasy? Just take notice.

Now look at the person or situation again with the *intention* of seeing something differently. Start by asking yourself things like, "Do I really need to be angry with this woman? After all, she seems a bit fragile and confused. Perhaps she really needed those few extra minutes with the pharmacist. Can I have more empathy for her?" Or, "This traffic situation is out of my control. I'm stuck in it now, so I might as well relax. After all, the folks involved in the crash are having a much harder day than I am right now. I can be grateful it wasn't me in that crash."

Once you make these statements, check in with yourself again. Has your body relaxed a bit? Has your breathing slowed? Maybe your heart even cracked open when you turned your attention to the struggle of another, like the victims of the car accident. The point is, you made a shift simply by being willing to explore a different perspective of the circumstance that, moments ago, had you feeling frustrated or irritated. By doing this one little thing, you effectively prove to your brain you really do have the power to change your experience simply by changing your perception of it.

In the words of the late Wayne Dyer, one of my all-time favorite self-help gurus, "If you change the way you look at things...the things you look at change." Do you see it now? Can you see the possibilities this one concept opens up for you?

By now, you're aware of what's coming next—my third and most heart-opening dance with grief. Another suicide to survive and process, another sudden death complete with the added drama of a stand-off with local authorities to live and learn through. Fasten your seatbelt because this ride is about to get bumpy....

"Grief can be the garden of compassion. If you keep your heart open through everything, your pain can become your greatest ally in your life's search for love and wisdom."

— Rumi

PART THREE

LEO

CHAPTER 10

THE PENDULUM

Millions of people struggle alone with some form of mental illness, living in fear of the stigma, prejudice, and discrimination they would encounter should their handicap be discovered. Anxiety disorders alone affect roughly 20 percent of Americans at present, and those are just the documented cases. I suspect many more suffer in secret.

My husband Leo was one of those statistics. His larger-than-life and very masculine personality, along with the times we lived in, prevented him from seeking help for the various emotional disturbances that affected his daily life, making maintaining long-term relationships especially difficult. You may recognize yourself or someone you know in his story of struggle to control his progressing illness and resulting behaviors. Or perhaps you see yourself in my tendency to play the role of codependent spouse.

Sadly, this relationship dynamic has become pretty commonplace in many societies and is often viewed as something you just have to learn to live with. If my husband had only opened up and talked about his insecurities, perhaps they wouldn't have held such sway over him. If he had addressed that particular elephant in the room head-on, I believe things would have played out very differently. Of course, I have no crystal ball and cannot say with certainty he would still be with us, but I think after reading Leo's story, you will agree that keeping his biggest problems locked deep inside led to his death.

If only he had trusted me enough to share his pain, perhaps he could have let some of the poison drain out of himself instead of keeping it locked inside to grow and fester. If only he had trusted his own Soul enough to guide him through this life, perhaps he wouldn't have been filled with so much self-loathing. If only the email he sent to his district manager at work Sunday afternoon asking for professional help was answered before he woke the following Tuesday, perhaps he would have felt a tiny sliver of hope. If only.…

We can never truly know what goes on inside someone else's mind at any given moment, can we? Even when we think we know someone well, our perceptions are based on how we take in the information given to us and how we process it. And we cannot push help onto someone who isn't ready to accept it. In the case of my troubled husband Leo, things had progressed too far to turn back by the time he reached out for help.

Suicide will rock the foundation of the world we, as survivors, find ourselves living in, since the nature of the death tends to feel acutely intimate and often horribly violent, leaving gruesome imprints on our brains that can be difficult to get rid of. It can knock our internal compass out of whack, leaving us confused and baffled about what happened, our minds screaming, "Did this really just happen? Is it true? How can it be?" as we try to make sense of a world where people actually do this to themselves.

Since I had already lived through what society sees as the worst loss one could ever suffer—my child's horrifying death by suicide—surely I could survive this experience, right?

As you walk along with me through these next chapters, I'm asking you to exercise care in how you view and judge Leo's behavior. I truly believe he was suffering internally a great deal more than any of us ever realized, and I feel he deserves some compassion. You and I can give that to him now since I have come to understand how we are all connected by this unseen force of life flowing through the fabric of time, entwining us together for eternity. What you think and feel affects me on some level just like the ever-expanding ripples of a tiny pebble tossed into a pond disturbs the entire body of water. So, if you are able, please send a wish of compassion and healing to my love, who left this earth far too soon and for all the wrong reasons.

"I know the truth, that the Soul lives on.
I know the truth, that we are all ONE."

(Excerpt from the song, "Surviving the Storm" by Vicky Edgerly)

Dear Leo,

I'm reading a book about a woman who had to take her children and go into hiding to escape her abusive husband. Even though you've been dead for ten years, I still find myself a bit triggered when she describes her situation. Her husband's patterns of behavior mirror yours to a tee. I remember long, lovely periods of being romanced and cherished by you followed by a pattern of distancing and building tensions, always culminating in some type of over-the-top outburst or blowout that often involved violence in some form.

I was able to convince myself for many years it was not "abuse." It was certainly not the type of abuse you hear about where, like the heroine in my book, women have to literally run for their lives, staying hidden for their own safety and that of the young children they have in tow. No, who was I to complain about a man whose only faults were a taste for alcohol, a bad temper, and a sharp tongue?

You made things hard for me, Leo, and there just isn't any way to sugarcoat that. I didn't think our marriage would survive after nine stress-filled months of caring for my dying daughter in our home. You confessed at the end you didn't really believe she was dying. I'm not sure how you came to accept such a thing as truth, what with all the nurses coming and going to change dressings and increase her pain meds. I'm not sure how you missed all the suffering and the way her body gave up every ounce of flesh before finally succumbing to death, but somehow you did.

And I still, to this day, do not understand how you justified your atrocious behavior toward me, a mother spending every second of her free time nursing her only surviving child through a grueling and extremely painful demise. Your cruel comments and unreasonable demands at a time when I was calling upon every ounce of personal strength I had just to be able to face each day only added to my sense of despair.

Maybe the grief was too much for you. Maybe you just weren't wired to shoulder a burden as heavy as this one. Maybe all the additional activity in our home disrupted your ability to cope with daily life, adversely affecting your various mood swings. Maybe.

But, honey, why didn't you just say so? Why on earth did you wholeheartedly agree to bringing my daughter home to die? Why, at any point during her stay, didn't you simply tell me the stress was more than you could handle? I would have understood—I would have found a way to make it easier for you. I would have had I been given the chance.

Of all the hurtful things you said to me during your frequent rage-filled outbursts, telling me I was "damaged goods" because my son took his own life was the most painful. I had to work really hard, you know, not to take those words into my being. I had to call upon all my superpowers to keep my mind pushing back against that especially nasty barb to keep it from becoming my truth.

You also made it a point to tell me, quite often I might add, that even though I seemed to handle my son's death better than people expected, I would not, you were quite sure, be as able to adapt to losing my daughter. You fully expected me to crumble after her death. But I did not. It did not break me like you thought it would (hoped it would?).

I never quite figured out why you behaved in those particular ways. Was it the attention she got from others while she was sick? I know it angered you. You'd rant and rave about how unfair it was for her to be showered with so much love, affection, and of course, gifts. You claimed she was undeserving. You'd recite over and over all the ways she fell short as a mother, a woman, a member of society. And if you sensed I disagreed with you in any way, you'd make sure to include accusations toward me, her mother, for raising such a waste of a human being.

The thing you didn't know is I knew you, Leo. I knew you needed this period of steam venting. I loved you through most of those stress-relieving tirades. I did. I saw your own pain over feeling helpless. You, the man with knight-in-shining-armor syndrome who had nothing to offer by way of help to your damsel in distress. You saw other people offering me the comfort and physical aid you could not give, and it triggered your own insecurities. I saw you, Leo; I did.

And even though I loved you with everything I had, when your rage grew to giant proportions, when you could no longer contain it and it grew bigger than the both of us, in those moments I would know true fear.

When your eyes became black as coal, when all light and sparkle had gone from them, you became a dead, soulless thing to me. Try as I might, when you were inches from my face, screaming horrible accusations and hurling the most hateful comments you could think of, always forcing me to look into those vacant eyes while you delivered each blow, I could not love you, Leo. I could not love you when you needed it most because fear moved in and pushed love aside.

You tried to lay the responsibility at my feet, and for a while I accepted it. After all, isn't it the wife's role to hold up her exhausted and stressed-out husband? Shouldn't she be supportive in all ways, especially if he is struggling with something internally?

You'd beg me at the height of your anger to tell you I loved you. "Just wrap your arms around me, Vic, and tell me you love me, and all this will go away now." That's what you'd say—right on the heels of telling me I was nothing and would never amount to anything without you. After calling me a slut and whore and tearing down every feature of my personality and physical appearance, you'd cry out for my love. And when you ran out of things to sling at me directly, you'd tear into those I loved like my dead and dying children, beloved friends, and family.

I could always see the shift in your posture just before you'd speak those words. It happened as soon as you ran out of made-up insults. First, you took great care in bringing up each and every thing I'd ever told you about myself in confidence, using my closely guarded secrets as weapons. Once you had spent your stock of hate and degradation, you'd reach a crossroads, and at that intersection, you'd have a choice. In those moments, you'd ask for my love because that truly would have ended each episode with you dissolving into my embrace where you would marvel and rejoice at your good fortune for having such a wonderful woman at your side.

But I was out of my league, Leo. I had no idea how to help you. I didn't even know how deep your problems ran, where they originated, or even how they presented inside your head because you never shared that with me. You never shared your insecurities. You came close but were never able to open yourself up to being vulnerable that way. Looking back, I can see why you'd want to keep your secrets to yourself. As someone who collected another's most vulnerable truths to use as ammunition against them later, I imagined you would have assumed everyone behaved that way, so you protected your own at all costs.

Perhaps having Tierra in the house with her endless entourage of nurses, caregivers, friends, and family coming and going made you feel too exposed. Perhaps you feared having so many people around would lead others to eventually discover who you really were underneath the shining example of a doting husband you projected for the rest of the world to see.

You kept up the charade for a long time. You kept playing the role of helpful, compassionate, and loving partner. You even doted on Tierra now and then to "give me a much-deserved break." You kept it up... until you couldn't.

Remember how you'd tell me, over and over again, during Tierra's illness that her death would be the one to undo me? You'd insist I couldn't survive it—that grieving the loss of my only surviving child would be too much for me to bear. But no, Leo, it was your death that almost did me in. You see, grief after losing each of my kids may have temporarily dampened my joy in this life but you, Leo, you threatened to plunge the light that is my eternal Soul into total darkness.

Luckily, I learned much more about you after your death. I saw your vulnerability more clearly. In death, my love for you returned pure and perfect like it was originally intended to be. In death, my safety was no longer in question. In death, I could feel your love without fear whispering in my ear to be wary. In death, you set me free.

After delivering my daughter safely to her grave, I told you one day you would have to sit and hear my words. If our marriage had any hope of survival at all, I would need to tell you exactly how your actions affected me during Tierra's illness and how they stayed with us. Listening to hard truths about yourself was something I knew you had never done before and would find extremely difficult to do.

I was surprised, yet still a bit doubtful when you came to me a mere month or so after Tierra died and said you were ready to listen and open to hearing what I had to say. How could I not love you when you sat so patiently and gave me your attention without interruption as I waded through all the ways you had hurt me over the months, eventually wrapping me up in one of those hugs you were so well known for—the ones that make the recipient feel completely and utterly safe, protected, and loved?

I loved you then, Leo. I loved you for allowing. You had nothing you could offer by way of apology or explanation, but you had that hug, and you gave it freely. I loved you then but with resignation. Resignation because I knew this was just a moment in time. I would cherish it, but in the end, it would make no difference in the path we were both on. We had gone well past the point of no return, and I think we both knew it then.

What a contradiction you were, Leo. While I can never forget all the ways you were cruel and demeaning, I also remember all the ways you were loving and giving. I don't know what the world at large would have labeled you since you would never consent to any professional help or diagnosis, but it felt to me like bipolar disorder. At any rate, I could clearly see you swinging like a pendulum, and when you were high, life was good—really, really good. And when you swung low, life for those around you got very dark.

The first few months after Tierra's death floated by like a dream. I finally had my doting husband back at my side. Things lightened for both of us the day she released her body and flew. The shift was quite marked, and you and I entered a new honeymoon period of sorts. At least for a little while.

For a time, things looked promising. But I saw you, Leo. I saw you begin to struggle as the weeks turned into months and your dance with alcoholism demanded more and more of your attention. The pendulum had begun its inevitable downswing.

I watched you losing ground with your battle to resist the drink, easily stumbling upon your various hiding places, a beer or two in the little barn fridge or a six-pack under the tarp at the woodpile confirming my impression our newly rekindled love affair would soon crumble under the weight of your demanding addictions.

I wasn't terribly surprised when I returned to my car one day after facilitating an event a couple of towns away to find several messages from you on my phone, each becoming more and more frantic and difficult to understand as I listened.

I could make out that an escalating family drama was causing you to become more and more agitated and angry as I toggled through the disjointed voicemails you left. At some point, you adopted a "fuck it" attitude and went "all in," switching from beer to vodka. That part was obvious in the incoherent, word-slurring monologues toward the end of those delivered to my phone. There was no turning back now. The pendulum was picking up speed.

While I sat listening to your recorded tirades, two things happened to me: 1) I immediately felt fear because I had no idea what I'd be walking into when I got home, and 2) it suddenly became clear I could no longer stay with you. Things were never going to change. If anything, they would continue to deteriorate until one or both of us ended up dead. In those quiet moments alone in my car, I knew that to be true. So, I steeled myself and drove home to face what would come.

I knew things were bad when I found our house guest's belongings bagged up and thrown out onto the road in front of our driveway. I also knew I was in big trouble. But I still believed if I just went in and let you tell your story without interrupting as a sign of my support, I'd somehow be okay.

You made it easy for me that day, Leo. For that I am eternally grateful. It was still quite frightening for me since you were far more inebriated than I had ever seen you by the time I got home. I used what reserves I had left, the remnants of who I was before we became "us," remnants that were still alive somewhere deep inside. I listened to your clumsy attempts to spin a convincing tale of how wronged you had been and how deserving your various victims were of the things you set in motion with the drunken phone calls you made that day that could never be taken back.

My mind and heart were numb in that last hour we lived together as husband and wife in our beautiful home in the woods. I felt detached and far away, void of all emotion as you spent the last vestiges of your rage, closing the gap between us, leaving me no choice but to endure the penetrating gaze of your black, soulless eyes as they bore into mine one last time, eventually clouding over as you lost the ability to retain interest in your own distorted narrative.

My lack of capacity to feel in those moments left me with quiet clarity and a confident resolve I did not know I possessed. It had all become clear. I just had to wait for you to pass out. Then I would hide your truck keys because even in the midst of this life-changing drama, I didn't want you hurting yourself or anyone else should you decide to try to follow me. Once you were sprawled out on the bed, oblivious to the world, I made my escape without so much as an overnight bag.

As I drove off the property, I could see the ghost of who you were all those years ago when the house was brand new and full of promise. I saw you standing at the mailbox with me, giving me this instruction, as if it were the key to the universe itself in its importance and reverence. You said, "Vic, if ever things get too dark, just walk me to this mailbox and tell me to stop and look at all we have, all we've created together, and everything will reset itself. I promise."

I believed you then, and for a time, that ritual had some effect—for a time. But on that day, Leo, you did not remember to walk to the mailbox as you had vowed to do all those years ago, and things did not reset themselves as you had said they would.

On that day, you crossed a threshold you could never return from. On that day, I didn't know that the next time I'd set foot on our private, nine-acre lot in the woods, I'd be wearing a new title, no longer your wife but your widow.

As I drove away, I was unable to exhale fully at first, taking short, panting breaths. I eventually found myself at my sister's place after stopping for toiletries and a couple of days' worth of clothes at the local Walmart. I felt deeply exhausted—the kind of exhaustion I felt after Adam died, the kind that threatens to put your light completely out once and for all. I turned my phone off that night and slept like the dead.

Taking steps to leave the abusive relationship my marriage had become was one of the most frightening things I had ever done. The day I left my husband passed out from alcohol and stole away to my sister, Linda's house marked a turning point for me that I knew would usher in monumental changes. Of course, I had no idea my actions would prompt Leo's desire to commit suicide, and for this, I am most grateful because if I had seen that coming, I most likely would not have taken the necessary steps to extricate myself from what I believed was a dangerous situation.

I'd like to think I had grown enough as a person by then to make this life-altering choice for the sake of my own safety and wellbeing, but admittedly, I had not. No, the decision to do the hard thing and walk away with no belongings, no money, and no plan was a leap of faith I found the courage to make on behalf of my granddaughter, Skyla, whose life with us would have gotten much, much worse as Leo's alcoholism would surely accelerate as he aged.

Over time, I forgave myself for not caring enough about *me* to get out of that situation long before things became so critical, and I've finally learned to love myself through and through. But it took some time and, again, *conscious effort* to relieve myself of the burden of all the character assassination Leo had visited on me.

This glimpse into our volatile relationship dynamics serves a purpose beyond story construction and narrative. I've included it because it will speak directly to the hearts of those who struggle with what I call "complex grief," where the grieving process is not quite straightforward but often interrupted by complicated relationship issues not fully resolved before the other died.

Is this you? Did someone you know die leaving unfinished relationship business? Are you experiencing additional angst over their death because of it? Are you struggling to come to terms with knowing the two of you will never resolve your issues? Do you feel anger toward them? Do you feel shame for feeling anger toward the dead?

As the coming chapters will show, all is not lost in these cases. Remember, the deceased still exists as a disembodied Soul. Because they still exist, it's not too late to work on relationship issues with them through practiced ADC (after-death communication). For example, writing heartfelt apologies for things you have done in a letter to your deceased or visiting a reputable psychic medium in hopes of receiving the apology they could never give while living can profoundly aid your quest to heal.

Let's take a look at the gifts I chose to see and accept during my own experience with a more complex grief journey. Consider whether I could have viewed my journey through Leo's suicide from this perspective if I had not already blazed a trail through the dark and distorted landscape of death and grief after losing my children.

"For each thorn, there's a rosebud…
For each twilight – a dawn…
For each trial – the strength to carry on…
For each storm cloud – a rainbow…
For each shadow – the sun…
For each parting – sweet memories when sorrow is done."

— Ralph Waldo Emerson

CHAPTER 11

THE GRIM REAPER RIDES SHOTGUN

One of the first things Leo said on the phone an hour before he killed himself was to wonder if he was doing the right thing by telling me his plan. While in his most raw and vulnerable frame of mind he still realized he was potentially undoing me mentally, saddling me forever with being the last person to talk with him and the one who failed to save his life.

Even without direct involvement in the event, survivors of another's suicide will obsessively search to identify who is to blame. We erroneously assign fault to those we feel could have or should have behaved differently toward the deceased lest we turn our contempt inward and take on the overwhelming guilt of their decision to die ourselves.

Having a front row seat to my husband's suicide left me many opportunities to decide whether or not to accept any blame. Of all the recurring questions I asked myself in the weeks and months that followed, "Could I have saved him?" is the one that threatened to haunt me the most.

The scene ahead is quite intense, so I hesitated before deciding to include it in this book, thinking it might be too graphic for some. But in the end, I saw great value in showing you exactly what takes place in the mind of someone who has chosen to employ conscious living methods when faced with such a traumatic event. Time and again, I would see-saw between human emotion, which threatened my sanity, and periods of peace where I *knew* I would be okay.

You, too, are about to have a front row seat, witnessing the moment of Leo's death through my eyes—eyes that toggled between human reaction and spiritual faith. Take my hand; we'll watch it unfold together....

(Dear Leo cont.)

Of course, you were first and foremost on my mind when morning arrived and everything came rushing back. Along with all the poignant memories from the night before came the feelings I had yet to allow myself to experience. Hours passed before I turned on my phone and listened to all the desperate messages you left after waking to find me and your truck keys gone.

I knew how you were feeling then, my Leo, and just like the Grinch on Christmas Day, my heart swelled with compassion for you. I knew you'd be tearing into yourself as memories of the things you had said and done to those you loved the day before came into focus. You would hate yourself beyond belief, allowing the all-consuming shame to be your undoing.

When I finally felt I could talk to you without falling into my codependent pattern of "forgiving and forgetting" to restore order to the world, you seemed relieved I agreed to meet you. I couldn't help but feel dread, knowing the meeting would not go as you were hoping. I would not be smiling and agreeing to come home with you. Not this time, Leo.

You looked completely broken that day, at Burger King of all places. Somehow, the place made you look much older and smaller than when we last saw each other, less than twenty-four hours before. My heart broke for you, Leo. I know you were aware of that. You'd tell me so yourself on your last day. You'd tell me you knew I loved you all along. You'd tell me you finally saw me, really saw me for how beautiful I truly was as a person, a friend, and a wife. You would tell me on the day you died, but it was too late then to alter what had already been set in motion.

When we parted ways in the BK parking lot that day, you were a mere shell of the man I had fallen so deeply in love with so many years before. You were resigned to the reality of the situation. You agreed with me it was not safe for my granddaughter, whom we held precious guardianship over since her mother's death, to return from her vacation to our home. You had looked in the mirror and come face to face with what you had become, and you knew you were out of control.

It must have felt like an insurmountable loss to you. Even though I sat across from you over half-eaten burgers and fries at the table and handed you a perfectly viable plan to help us through those difficult times. I was offering you one more year of my life. One full year of my devotion and attention, provided you would agree to addiction counseling for yourself and marriage counseling for us.

In the meantime, Sky and I would find our own place so we could begin to feel safe again in our own home. We could relearn how to relax and fall asleep at night without anxiety meds or sleep aids. We could leave a sock on the floor, spill a glass, or forget to close a cabinet door without fearing we might be found out and chastised or punished by you. We could begin to heal.

You said you understood completely. You said you believed it was the best way forward. So, what changed your mind, Leo? Or were you just paying lip service at that point, assuming I'd come around to your way of thinking in a day or two? It didn't make any sense to me when, thirty-six hours later, you had my full attention on the phone as you ratcheted a round into the chamber of the 9mm handgun you carried everywhere with you, the same gun I had held while contemplating my own suicide after Adam's death a decade before.

I woke that Tuesday morning feeling just a little bit lighter—I wouldn't say hopeful yet. That word wasn't quite within my grasp, but I definitely did not feel quite so hopeless. I believed what you told me at Burger King on Sunday afternoon. I believed you would fight along with me to save our marriage. I believed in you, Leo. I did.

I was anxious to get on the road to work that morning so I could call you from the car. The commute from Linda's place would give us the better part of an hour to chat. I was hoping to hear something in your voice that would quell my angst over how you were processing all this because I knew it could go one of two ways. I knew it all depended on where the pendulum was in the never-ending, ever-repeating cycle of rising and falling.

I'm not sure how much of this you were internally aware of, but I had learned your highs and lows were very much married to each other. In other words, if your pendulum of emotion swung really high, you'd be on top of the moon for a time. Life would be rich and full with adventure around every corner. Then, the following drop would be equal in measure, resulting in events matching in intensity but on the polar opposite end of the emotional spectrum, creating a world without light and packed with hidden danger.

On that day as I dialed your number, I hoped you were already on the upswing. After all, we had a plan for moving forward together, and I assumed that would give you what you needed to feel better about things. I had grand illusions of using the next year to do some really deep healing work within myself while simultaneously rebuilding our relationship. I had romantic notions of rekindling the magic we once were as a couple. I had dreams, Leo, and they included you.

But I heard a different story when you picked up the line that morning. I heard the voice of a stranger. The man who answered the phone was old, really old. That man was ancient and worn down like an old car that could barely spitter and sputter to life every morning. I did not recognize you in that voice. I did not hear my Leo in those early moments of our last conversation on that fateful day.

My heart sank once more as I listened to your desperate pleas. The cadence of your speech was manic, listing all the reasons I should abandon my plan to find safe housing for Sky and me and return home to you instead. I could send Sky back to Plymouth, you said, condemning the child to the mother-like role to RyLee and Qwynn she had been cast into upon her mother's death that you insisted we rescue her from to raise as our own.

You begged me to believe in your ability to make things better for us just one more time. It would work if I would just give you the chance. But, Leo, you knew I could not do that. You knew I could not and would not abandon that child. You knew. And you were prepared. You knew what the outcome would be, but you had to try one last time.

What I heard in your voice then was authentic desperation, as opposed to the manipulative play-acting version you often used to woo me into submission after one of your more damaging pendulum swings. The full-scale truth of that became clear pretty quickly.

After calmly repeating myself and reminding you of all we agreed to that day at Burger King, you eventually heard the finality of my words, and you made the shift. The energy of it was a palpable thing—large and looming, dark and sinister, and it traveled with me as an uninvited passenger in the car for what seemed like an eternity.

"Are you sure, Vic? Are you absolutely sure you will not come home to me today? I love you, Vic!"

Remember how you asked that of me over and over while purposely allowing me to hear you pop the clip into your 9mm and ratchet a round into the chamber, so sure I'd know exactly what your intent was? After all, that wasn't the first time you'd pulled that piece out in my presence during an emotionally charged event, was it, Leo?

To this day, I do not know how you imagined things would play out. Perhaps you'll make it clear in a message from beyond the grave.

Perhaps I won't know until we meet again after my own life here is finished, but I wondered about it then. I wondered if it was all a big bluff designed to tug so hard on my heartstrings that I would be yanked right back into your world. I wondered if I'd overreacted and, with my own actions, somehow sealed your fate. I did. I wondered those things then.

But if it was a bluff, you neglected to build yourself an escape route, Leo. In the car that day through my phone, I heard you quickly shift into your confident, authoritative self. You made demands of me, "Don't come to the house, Vic. I don't want you to come here. Once we hang up, call the police, and send them, but don't you come."

"No! I'll come now," I replied. "We can talk. You'll see. Together, we can make a plan for fixing our relationship. But it will take time, and it is not safe for me, and I will not abandon my grandchild. You know I cannot!"

Back and forth it went, for how long I do not remember. An hour? Five minutes? An eternity...that's how long it was, an eternity. For an eternity we went back and forth between you insisting, "This has to happen; I have no choice," and me trying to use reason to convince you otherwise, eventually collapsing into a blubbering mess, crying and begging you not to do this thing to yourself, your family...to us.

Neither of us would hang up. In long periods of silence, I could hear your breath, and you could most certainly hear my remaining sobs and sighs between rounds of pleading for your life and your insistence that I hang up so you could get on with it.

I don't know how I pulled my focus together long enough to notice the battery on my cell phone was about to die. The realization of what that meant made my blood run cold. I started a new, frantic chant, "Leo! My battery is going to die! I don't have a charger in my car. My phone is going to go dead! I am not going to hang up, but my phone is going to die!"

"Hang up, Vic. Hang up now, and this all ends."

"No! I can't! I won't!" I insisted.

The tables had been turned. I was the one losing my shit while you remained calm, cool, and collected. The police chief would tell me the same thing a few hours later. He said you were perfectly calm and reasonable, and you even chuckled with him over the current state of political affairs the world was in at the time, citing specific ways our current president was ruining our country.

It's funny how your mind becomes detached from your circumstance in high-stress situations. I'd once read that this is a defense mechanism, and I can recall falling back on it a lot after Adam's death. It's like if we check out mentally, an autopilot system, which I believe is my soul, kicks in like an automatic generator does when the power goes out during a nasty storm. I believe that was what happened to me next. While a big part of me was definitely "checked out," another, more primal part was ready to act.

By that point in our conversation, I had pulled off at Happy Family Restaurant and parked, no longer able to concentrate on driving. I was not consciously aware of anything outside my vehicle, focused only on you, my dying phone, and that wretched "thing" that was riding shotgun with me, that unseen passenger who, in hindsight, I realize must have been The Grim Reaper.

For some reason, my gaze ventured beyond the emotional prison you held me in just in time to see a police car cruise by on the road in front of me. In that instant, I knew the situation was too big for me, so I followed, knowing only that I needed help. I thought they could help me save you, Leo.

I drove toward home, pulled into the Barnstead Police Department, and frantically scribbled your phone number, our address, and a note that read, "My husband has a gun and is going to kill himself…I need help!" all while simultaneously begging you not to do this and praying my phone's battery would hold out.

The police chief himself greeted me in the parking lot that day. I can only imagine what I must have looked like to him with tears and snot streaming down my face, which was contorted with pain, agony, panic, and fear. I was desperate not to tip you off that I had contacted the police.

I didn't know what would happen once I reached out for help. I think I truly believed the police would somehow save you from yourself. Later, I chastised myself, "What did you think, Vic? Did you really believe they would waltz onto the property and wrestle him into submission? Or did you assume they would have the words needed to convince him not to do this terrible thing to himself when your own begging and pleading had no effect at all?"

At one point, I thought they might get a sniper to shoot you with a tranquilizer gun so you could be safely taken into custody. How foolish my thoughts were! It's like the traumatic situation I found myself in had once again short-circuited my brain's ability to think and reason normally, a phenomenon I had become quite familiar with after Adam's suicide.

That act of asking for help, in what a therapist would later describe as "an impossible situation," would become a focal point for a lot of hate directed my way after your death—hate from those who loved you before you and I were an us. Those who never got to know me because you kept them all at bay, off in the distance of our peripheral vision where they could not get close enough to see the reality of who you had become at the hands of your decades' long struggle with alcoholism and emotional disturbances. For in those end days, Leo, it had become clear you were giving the reins over to your disease. You had given up and were spiraling.

"One of us has to hang up, Vic. I need you to do it. Hang up, Vic, then call the police. DON'T COME ON THE PROPERTY! Do you hear me?"

Time and again, you ran through these demands. Did you even hear me when I matched your cries with my own, begging you to understand my battery was going to die, and my phone would disconnect? I was terrified you'd think I had hung up. That you'd finish it all then, sure in the knowledge I would never dare disobey you and would have called the police immediately as instructed.

Now, more than ten years later, I struggle to remember all we said during that last hour we shared together on this earth. If I allow myself to swim in the memories, completely submerging myself, occasionally one will come close enough to the surface that I can see it clearly and make out what it has to say.

You spoke words to me that day I had longed to hear you say during our marriage but never thought you would. Words of acknowledgment for your part in how things had played out between us those last few years and led us to that point in space and time.

You told me you loved me over and over, and you'd finally realized how much I truly loved you, which apparently you could never quite believe until those last few moments on the phone. You also said you had trusted me more than any other human being, and to me that was the highest compliment of all because I knew you trusted no one…ever.

I can watch those memories float by today, calling the ones near that I wish to spend more time with before sending them back to the depths of my subconscious, eventually to be stored away in the long-term-memory vaults of my mind until the day my name is called to leave this world behind and experience my own life review before moving on to the other realms of the afterlife.

But on that day, all I could hear in your words were goodbyes. Every heartfelt sentiment on your part only conveyed to me just how real and final this situation was, all those nouns and verbs melting together to say only one thing…"Goodbye, Vic."

I heard the shot, you know. After my phone had gone dead, I could no longer tolerate just sitting in the police station parking lot as the chief had insisted, so I headed toward home. But when I got to the top of our secluded dirt road, emergency vehicles had blocked my path, and try as I might, they would not let me, your wife, through to the property. "You must wait here," they said, insisting it wasn't safe to get any closer.

Sitting alone in my car, where time rushed by at a dizzying speed yet stood still all at once, I remember most the deafening silence...and then the shot. I thought, *No, that couldn't be it.* The sound was much too small, more like a firecracker kids light off on the Fourth of July. Just a puny little "pop" really. But yes, I knew it was the shot. It just seemed odd to me—the sound of someone ending their own life should be loud and carry far and wide like the pain-filled chaotic existence the survivors are left with does.

I closed my eyes and tried to reach out to you with my mind, my heart, my whole being. I tried to touch your spirit in that moment like I could easily do with my kids. But I couldn't sense you at all, couldn't feel anything. So, I hoped. I hoped I was wrong.

Time continued to speed by, but inside my car it halted, the air thick like molasses slowing everything down to a crawl. I waited for someone to come bring me the news, already beginning to accept what would or would not happen next.

First, I saw a police cruiser leave our driveway. It drove slowly up the road, stopped at the intersection where I was parked, and then continued through toward town. I noticed it did not have its emergency lights on. My first thought was, *Well, it's over.* I realized they didn't seem to be in a hurry, so I knew you were not hurt and being rushed to the hospital. I thought maybe, just maybe, they had you in custody. But the windows of the cruiser were darkened, and I could not see if you were sitting in the back. I hoped anyway.

In my distress, I failed to notice my unwanted passenger, the Reaper, was no longer in the car with me. His business was with you, so he had taken his leave without so much as a "Thank you for the ride."

I didn't know until the police chief stood next to my vehicle, waiting for me to open my window. To hear him say, "Mrs. Ellis, I'm sorry, but he did it. Your husband killed himself," was like a physical blow that completely knocked the wind out of me. I couldn't breathe for a moment. It was as if I had forgotten how. But then I did take a breath. And with the exhale came the panic and a flood of hot tears. I put my head on the steering wheel, and in a moment of surrender, let them flow.

I felt defeated but strangely enough also relieved. Relieved the waiting was over. The horrible, unbearable waiting. Waiting alone in the darkness that had threatened to engulf me and drag me under that day, taking with it the last vestiges of the sanity I was so desperately trying to hold onto.

Immediately after came the guilt. How could I possibly feel relieved at a time like this? My husband, my love, my best friend had just shot and killed himself.

Where were you in those first few moments, Leo? Because I couldn't feel your presence until I was allowed back on the property a couple of hours later. In the midst of the shock and drama unfolding around me, I was startled and amazed to discover you were speaking directly to my mind, telling me how much you loved me, asking me to forgive you, and warning me there'd be "one more" I'd have to endure in this lifetime.

I thought that last message a bit foreboding and went on to struggle with worry and paranoia over the possibility of facing another great loss sometime soon. It must have been a year or two after your death before I finally found peace with the inevitability of that happening at some point in my life, something I'd never be able to change, so I was finally able to let it go.

I have to ask, as I've often wondered, did you see me, Leo? Did you see me when I knelt on the soft, pine-scented forest floor next to your drying blood on the very day you died and offered reiki healing to you, and the dogs nearby in their kennel, and the land itself for having witnessed such a violent act? Could you feel how much love I had for you then? In all that has transpired between us, that one question would hang in the air until you answered it through a psychic medium I had the pleasure of sitting with a couple of years later. Then you thanked me for "the gift of love I offered you the day you died."

"I watched you drop down to your knees, and I felt your love
wash over me, yes Darlin' I did see."

(Excerpt from the song, "Did You See Me?" by Vicky Edgerly)

That was a tough chapter to read, wasn't it? Thank you for sticking it out. Quietly bearing witness to another's pain is one of the kindest, yet most powerful things we can do for each other. If what you see and hear within this book sparks even the slightest curiosity within you to explore a deeper understanding of your own grief journey, whether you are actively traveling it now or expect to at some point in the future, you have bestowed the greatest honor on me I can imagine. You will have benefited from my experiences and my willingness to share them, giving the deaths of my family even more meaning than I ever imagined.

By the time my husband chose to leave the world behind, I had developed a strong faith in myself and the unseen world of Spirit available to me, so contact with him came swiftly and easily from the very beginning. Still, I would enjoy sessions with a trusted psychic medium where I would always receive bits of information that served to confirm that what I thought I was experiencing was, indeed, an ADC (after-death communication).

Furthermore, since a trained medium has honed their skill to expert levels, they were able to provide complete thoughts, stories, and fully-formed messages from my deceased family members, whereas I had been mostly picking up on random signs, synchronicities, and broken sentences I would then have to interpret. It's like the difference between diagnosing a problem with your brakes because you heard a scraping noise and getting a skilled technician to take a look and advise you on exactly which parts need replacing. You get a much more detailed picture, and the information proves more helpful in addressing the problem.

Even so, I do not recommend the newly bereaved seek immediate audience with a psychic medium *unless* they are already accustomed to this type of service. Why? Because, if you recall, the brain's normal processes have been interrupted with the shock and trauma of the event, which leaves you in an extremely fragile and vulnerable state. Unfortunately, many folks out there practice mediumship without *integrity*.

Integrity in mediumship means the practitioner has studied their craft intensively (and is not just "practicing" on you to gain experience) and understands the sacredness of the process. They treat the sitter with reverence and compassion always, never using their craft to instill fear or sensationalize the process for personal gain in any way. They will never expand on any given message of their own volition to make the sitting more "profitable"; instead, they will stick to relaying exactly what they are receiving through their "clair" skills (clairvoyance—gift of sight, clairalience—psychic sense of smell, clairaudience—ability to hear, etc.).

I typically recommend folks wait at least six months before sitting with a medium for the first time. Wait longer if your grief symptoms are still acute. As you can imagine, hearing personal details and messages directly from your dead child or lover for the first time can result in some pretty mixed feelings. Those feelings might confuse you if you haven't given your brain a little time to heal and your understanding of the grieving process to develop. Approaching your first sitting with a less chaotic state of mind will help ensure a beautiful reading you'll be better equipped to receive and benefit from.

Furthermore, I don't recommend relying on a google search for a psychic medium; instead, reach out to family, friends, and coworkers for recommendations. (You might be surprised by how many people you know have used mediums!) If you cannot find a personal reference, my go-to list for tried-and-true mediumship (tested for legitimacy but not necessarily rated for integrity) can be found on Bob Olson's website at: https://bestpsychicmediums.com/thelist.htm

Please explore this option with an open heart and open mind. Then you will find just the right experience for you. I promise!

CHAPTER 12

THROUGH DEATH WE LEARN HOW TO LIVE

While I was dealing with the aftermath of Leo's choices, I cussed him out for exercising his power to control me one last time. Of course I did. I cursed him for forcing me to be part of it, understanding I most likely would have to work through some damage left by the shocking event that belongs on one of those surreal true crime shows, not on our beautiful property nestled in the woods of New Hampshire. But once the first few intense weeks passed, the grief settled into the familiar process of ebb and flow I had become accustomed to. The only visible damage the trauma left me with was a slightly noticeable facial tic I was able to release simply by acknowledging it and spending some time with purposeful relaxation techniques.

I am amazed I don't have a fear of gunfire or any triggering flashback memories of the horrible day I heard the shot that ended my husband's life. I truly expected to have to work through some level of PTSD after living through that nightmare. While I cannot offer you scientific proof, only my own impressions of what I was experiencing, I believe it was my ever-evolving spiritual beliefs and practices that prepared me to walk through such an event without it damaging me beyond repair. "The proof is in the pudding," as they say, and the result here is I do not walk through life saying, "Ever since that day I can no longer ______________." (Fill in the blank with any number of things people no longer enjoy after living through shocking or traumatic events.)

Once the police had taken what control they could over the situation, I refocused my attention on what was happening around and within me. I found myself shifting between human emotion, predominately love, affection, and worry for my husband, and seeing the bigger picture of a Soul contract playing out.

One thing that surfaced again and again in my mind during those endless moments waiting for the inevitable was something Leo had said frequently since Adam's death. After admiring how I chose to process my grief by throwing myself into my spiritual studies and research, he often said, "It's *you* I want by my side when I go, Vic. Of everyone else in the whole world, I want you to be with me when I die."

Recalling his wishes in that profound moment prompted me to remember all I had learned about Soul Contracts and how we form alliances with other Souls before incarnating into any given lifecycle to learn together the lessons an earthly life can offer. So, was this coming into play for Leo and me? Was it possible it was our destiny all along for things to end this way?

I've come to believe while we are born with a certain path laid out before us, a roadmap of our lives, if you will, we are also sovereign beings by nature and come equipped with free will so that at any given time, our own Soul can step in and alter the trajectory of our life. Believing my Soul is in absolute control has allowed me to remain somewhat calm while things played out on our property that bright summer day. Somewhere deep inside me, I knew Leo and I had agreed to see this thing through together, and now the day it would all come to pass had arrived, so I vowed to stay as close to his side as circumstances would allow.

In the midst of that chaos, I was able to draw on everything I had learned after Adam's death, giving me confidence in my ability to handle whatever came my way, secure in the knowledge my Soul knew how to walk me through the most treacherous landscape I would ever find myself in. Because of this mental "readiness" I seemed to have acquired, I found myself toggling between visceral, heart-stopping pain and a soft, quiet "knowing" that all would be well within me, even after such an experience.

I couldn't help noticing the similarities and differences in how I responded to what was happening compared to ten years earlier when Adam had died. Remember those numb-bubbles I believed were pockets of time where my mind simply couldn't handle any more pain and anguish so it would sort of "check out" while my body ran on autopilot? Turns out I was right. Those were times my Soul was stepping forward to take the reins when I could not. Here it was happening again, only this time I was consciously aware of it and engaged in the process, actively following its recommendations and advice while trusting it completely to see me through.

Let me sum it up like this. Since I took the time to explore the nature of the Soul and develop a close connection to mine, I was able to use this newfound ally to aid me when circumstances seemed too overwhelming for my puny human self. My belief that the Soul is a powerful and loving essence directly connected to the Source of all that is (God, the Universe, Life-Force energy—whatever you choose to call it) allowed me to relax into my grief journey after Leo died without the fear of losing my mind like I experienced after my son left.

I still felt the pain of loss, of course, but I had come to understand it and how it would move through me as long as I allowed it. Denying or fighting it would only result in holding on to it, keeping it with me or even burying it deep inside my body. Now I understand it's just an energy, something fluid and malleable I could allow to pass through me like ocean waves swelling and crashing on the beach.

And like an ocean wave will eventually recede, exposing all sorts of previously buried shells and tiny sea creatures, my waves of grief, once spent, would leave me standing on somewhat wobbly ground, looking around at a landscape I hardly recognized. Without the fear, my mind was free to understand that among the debris scattered on the ground around me were buried treasures just waiting to be discovered.

This is the saving grace for those of us willing to explore the possibility of an afterlife, a most valuable gift available to us all. When we accept it, we discover the disembodied Soul of our deceased loved one no longer dons a shroud of perverted thoughts and behaviors, but instead, shines brightly with a vibration of love and support. It's no longer just about survival for us because our curiosity will lead to some pretty wonderful discoveries when we give it the freedom to roam and discover new ways to look at things.

Some of us have trouble trusting our first experiences of contact with the deceased since our bodies may still be reacting with the very basic fight-or-flight responses we became so accustomed to when encountering a person who has continually threatened our wellbeing. Given a little time and with some practice, our abilities to recognize the little signs will improve and our Soul connection will strengthen as we relax into the realization that they are no longer "toxic" in demeanor or intentions toward us.

How about you? Have you ever been left with regrets over conversations you never made time for or relationship troubles you didn't have a chance to mend before your loved one left the earth? Have you tried reaching out to them in hopes they will hear you and see what weighs on your heart? Do you sometimes feel like they are near but then convince yourself it is only your imagination, even though you could swear you just caught a whiff of their favorite cologne while sitting alone with your memories of them?

While I busied myself with all the preparations involved in giving Leo a beautiful sendoff, I was enjoying frequent and remarkable contacts with him in spirit form. I would sense and often *hear* him as he stayed close while I ticked off all the tasks on my list, like arranging his cremation and picking out a gravesite for him where he could watch over my two kids. He kept showing up, making himself known to me and others as the day we would honor him with a memorial service on our beautiful property approached.

My willingness to engage with him along with his apparent prowess at breaking through any barriers that separate the living from the dead allowed us to immediately begin working on healing our troubled relationship. Offering him reiki healing on the day he died served to open my heart right on the heels of an event that would normally close down the hearts of anyone experiencing what I did that day.

While I still felt immense pain and sorrow with frequent periods of emotional release, I also noticed an undercurrent of hope blooming within my being. I understood a brand new life was waiting for me out there. Of course, there were still things to process emotionally and adjust to physically, but I was able to lean into this grief journey with faith that a beautiful new life awaited me up ahead. All I had to do was keep moving forward, putting my trust in my own Soul to guide me.

Let's take a look at how this all unfolded for me as more and more understanding took root within me.

(Dear Leo cont.)

I've learned to love my story of tragic loss, Leo. I've learned to love the thing you were so sure would be my ultimate undoing. It wasn't easy. It took a while, but the sixty-year-old woman I am today has finally brought it onboard as a welcome passenger, the polar opposite of the uninvited one who rode with me that fateful day in August ten years ago.

Far from The Reaper, this new passenger, my life story of love, loss, and human triumph, is one I know will always travel with me, ensuring I am never left alone in this world. When I consider the woman I was in that story, I cannot help but fear for her, root for her, cheer for her, and finally, love her unconditionally and with everything I've got. The Reaper may have brought death to my door, but learning to love my story taught me how to truly live.

The process was grueling, fascinating, terrifying, exhilarating, burdensome, liberating, and on and on I could go since the grief storm is just that, a storm of emotion and thoughts whirring around at different speeds and intensities before settling into a giant pile of jumbled confusion at the feet of those stricken with it.

But for the curious, and I thank the powers that be that I am counted among them, the seemingly tedious process of sorting those thoughts and emotions, arranging them into some kind of order that makes sense to the Soul, may lead us to discover who we really are inside and what we are capable of. Rebuilding one's life after repeatedly having it torn to shreds has a way of shaping a person's perspective. When you're faced with such mountains to climb, the only way to succeed is to put one foot in front of the other and begin.

The first two weeks following your death flew by in a jumble of activity as I switched back and forth between work, planning and orchestrating your cremation, memorial service, burial, and cleaning up the house, barn, and property in preparation to receive everyone who needed to feel close to you for that one day of fellowship.

You always said you didn't want any type of funeral when it was your time, but that was one request I simply could not grant. You did at times concede by telling me I could lay you "out in the barn" if I really felt I must do something in your honor. And so, that's what I did, darlin'. I laid your cremated remains out in your beloved barn, built with your own hands, in the company of your dogs and surrounded by your most impressive collection of deer and moose antlers.

The day was gorgeous, perfectly complementing the little piece of paradise we'd carved out for ourselves. I could feel you beaming with pride as those who loved you came up the drive, some for the very first time, and were met with such a vibrant and lovely homestead, the woodsmoke from the firepit scenting the air like a heady incense, creating an atmosphere of quiet reverence as occasional showers of crackling sparks leapt from the flames, apparently on their own journey toward the heavens.

You were always such a big personality, so it came as no surprise to me that you'd make your presence known from beyond the veil in the most magical ways, leaving the living with a flood of warm emotion, knowing beyond any doubt they had just been touched by your love.

I'd like to thank you for that, Leo. Thank you for walking with me through all the tough stuff. Thank you for helping me as much as you were able to with your kids, whose pain and anguish was breaking my heart. Thank you for making us laugh when our minds threatened to snap from the frantic energy of our repeating thoughts of your grisly end, like the day we caravanned to the crematorium in Manchester to view your body before releasing it to the final process that would turn your flesh and bones to ash.

I'll never forget how quickly and completely we all shifted from our collective mood of dread in anticipation of the horrors we would see that day, me with your daughter in the passenger seat and your boys in their truck following behind us. I marvel to this day over the dead's ability to orchestrate such perfectly timed "messages" from beyond.

We certainly could not ignore the high school marching band that just happened to be practicing in a city park directly across the street from the crematorium when it broke out in a robust rendition of "Play That Funky Music" at the exact moment we were pulling into the parking lot.

Your daughter and I both looked at each other, first with dour faces pinched in pain and disbelief, followed within seconds by a rush of relief and hysterical laughter—we both knew this to be your way of breaking the mood and easing our tension. We had no doubt your hand was in this as anyone close to you would have memories of you dancing and singing to that song whenever you heard it, no matter where you were or what you were doing at the time. And if we needed confirmation that we were not imagining it, we got just that moments later when both your boys greeted us smiling and laughing, excitedly exclaiming, "Dad's here!"

In like fashion, you were not shy about making your presence known throughout that hauntingly beautiful day on our property once we all gathered to say goodbye.

Your daughter was deeply touched when, walking the trail down to the river you loved so much, her firstborn, your first grandchild, picked up a branch from the forest floor and started using it as a walking stick... an unusual thing for such a small child to do all on their own without being prompted.

Not everyone would have known the significance of this, but those closest to you did. Anyone who ever spent time with you in the woods knew you to walk with a stick. And while my three grandkids enjoyed many hikes with you, all walking with sticks you had procured for them and lovingly carved each of their initials into, your own little granddaughter had never experienced this ritual herself.

So, it was pretty amazing the child would think all on her own, without ever being shown, that picking up a branch and using it as a walking stick was the most natural thing in the world to do. I've often heard it said children under four are still very "connected" to the other realms—the unknown lands and dimensions from whence we all came, that they still sense more around them than what the rest of us can see, hear, and touch in our human form. I was so happy to learn about this story and the parting gift you'd left for your daughter and first grandchild to treasure forever, a divinely timed cellphone photograph of a perfectly formed orb floating near the little girl as she lingered at the river's edge, a splendid gesture of your love for that child, something you never quite got to convey while you were living.

Messages from you after you died were plentiful, and they always held wonderful nuggets of healing, hope, love, and support. I could often feel your excitement when I realized you were trying to communicate, but the first time I felt you pass through my physical body, I was horrified.

You see, I was quite accustomed to feeling one of my kids as they presented me with a strong "chill" or "rush" that started at the top of my head and raced all the way down to my toes in waves that left my whole body tingling. But when I felt that same type of electric energy travel down the left side of my body, leaving the right side completely void of any such sensation, it left me in a panic. I immediately cried out to you, "Oh, no! Am I feeling this only on one side because you shot yourself in the head and did devastating injury to your brain, resulting in this phenomenon?"

"No, Vic," your response came quickly and sure, accompanied by your patented chuckle. "I chose this unique way so you will always know it's me and not someone else visiting in these moments."

Oh, what a relief that was. To this day, while I don't hear from you nearly as often as I did in those early months, when I do, you never fail to announce your presence in this same way, which always brings a smile to my face and reminds me I am never alone. I've often wondered if our hundreds of conversations about my own otherworldly contacts with my kids somehow strengthened the connection between us so we could so readily communicate in these ways after your death. I think perhaps it did.

I felt your love when you came to me, especially at night as I lay my head down to sleep. I could sense you lying next to me, always with your back to me as you did in life, facing your reading lamp. I could see myself moving toward you. First, to touch your back, then your shoulder…then I'd move in close and slip my hand under your arm to your chest. I could feel my face against the skin of your back as I pressed my body close to yours. I could stroke your chest hair and kiss your neck. I could see and feel this so clearly. I knew you were really there. I knew you had come so I might experience that again…and again…and again.

After you first left, I had to let a lot of stuff surface—all the hurt, humiliation, shame, and anger buried deep inside me. I think I have let all, or at least most, of that come up. At times it felt like purging—vomiting up all those cancerous things inside me trapped in the cells of my body for years. But now, all that remains is my love for you. All I have left is love—and it is perfect.

For quite some time, these little interludes with your Spirit left me feeling a closeness with you we were never able to achieve here on the physical plane, and I eagerly looked forward to each and every visit as we mended our dysfunctional marital relationship from beyond the veil. But even so, there came a day when I understood I could not sustain these frequent visits that kept you here by my side, in my heart, and on my mind if I was to venture forward in search of the woman I was to become and the new life that was waiting for me.

Having an open communication line to the dead can sometimes come with its own set of "fallout" experiences. We are touching on one of those occasions now. Widowhood laid a host of new challenges at my feet, and I quickly became almost dependent on the frequent, and often intimate, contacts with my husband, Leo. For the most part, these interludes were comforting and left me feeling like I still had the very best of my life partner here with me as I forged my way in my new reality.

But sustaining the marital relationship with Leo kept me at odds with my goals to enter a new chapter, one I would need to walk alone. Over time, I began to feel restricted and almost "held back" from crossing the threshold into the new life I could see taking shape just up ahead. How was I to traverse this roadblock?

I immediately realized how to approach it, so I easily slipped into an attitude of *trust*. I trusted my Soul to see me through by showing me the adjustments I needed to make to accomplish what was best for me and my healing journey.

I also reached for what I consider the "Swiss army knife" of all tools in my arsenal—my ability to alter my experience by changing my perspective. I knew a shift in my perception was required in this situation, and soon, an opportunity to do just that presented itself.

Simply making the decision to trust and allow things to unfold in their own way releases the struggle, allowing life to ebb and flow all around us more fluidly and without restriction. If I had pushed back against my intuitive discovery that I was becoming too attached to my dead husband, things would have looked quite different for me because the metamorphosis I was going through would have been interrupted or even halted completely.

While some widows are quite content to live the rest of their days as "the surviving wife of," I was not. I wanted something more for myself and needed to be completely free to explore my options. But did that mean I would have to let Leo go completely? Would I have to push him out of my life after leaning on him all these months? We'll look at how this played out in this next chapter of our love story, where Leo himself dons the role of supporting actor while I take the lead.

CHAPTER 13

'TIL DEATH DO US PART?

I'll never forget the first time I was introduced as "Leo's widow." I was attending his mother's funeral. She passed just a few months after his death. I felt detached from the word as one of his sisters led me around the room, introducing me with that acclaimed title. I felt like an imposter. Widow? Me? I cried about that later in my hotel room as the truth of it sank in. I was indeed a widow.

Once named a widow, was I to wear that status forever? Would I always be Leo's widow, or would there be a cutoff point where I was no longer "the surviving wife" but simply Vicky? For a time, the title felt comforting, like wrapping myself in one of Leo's oversized chamois shirts that still smelled of pine forest and wood smoke, bringing up memories of his wonderful hugs. It also gave me a place in society to belong, unlike the total isolation I felt after Adam's death since no label is given to a parent who has outlived their child, no badge of honor to announce to the world what I had been through.

As you can imagine, the widow's journey came with its own unique set of trials. Even with the challenges our relationship faced, I felt the loss of my husband in every area of my daily life. When the grief over Adam's suicide got to be too intense, I could convince myself he was simply "away." Then my mind would relax and I could breathe again since I wasn't used to seeing my grown son every day anyway, giving me a moment of respite from the pain. When the sorrow over my daughter's pending death became too heavy for me to carry, I could lean on Leo, depending on where in the pendulum swing we were. But when you lose a spouse, there is no one on the other side of the bed when you wake in the middle of the night in the grips of an acute wave of grief, no one to turn to, no one to lean on.

In addition to the heartbreaking loss of friend, confidant, and lover, I'd also lost my life partner, so I was left to shoulder all the responsibilities of home, yard, and finances alone. While taking on Leo's share of the work around our large, secluded property exhausted me physically, it also gave me much pleasure to move about our acreage using his tools and keeping up with his chores. Eventually, I had to let go of some things that proved too much for me, like cutting and stacking firewood to heat the house in winter and keeping up with a large vegetable garden, but I did continue cutting the grass myself each week because bouncing around on his lawn tractor wearing his floppy, worn-out straw hat made me feel closer to him.

With all I had learned and experienced about the afterlife and how the departed Soul can continue to interact with the living, I still had doubts and insecurities, wondering if I was interpreting these encounters correctly, especially when concerning decisions I'd make about the house and property or my life in general. I kept reaching out to him, wondering if he saw me, wondering if he approved, and hoping I wasn't disappointing him in how I cared for our treasured homestead. He never failed to send me a sign of confirmation at just the right moment like a small female deer (his self-assigned spirit animal) stepping out of the woods at the edge of our property to look directly at me before moving back into the darkening forest at the exact moment I was reaching out to Leo to ask for support or coming to me himself in a dream to remind me it was time to change the water filter.

While I heartily enjoyed these contacts with him and the renewed closeness I felt toward my husband, I have to point out that building a continuing relationship with a loved one in Spirit can be both a blessing and a curse. The blessing, of course, is the opportunity to continue experiencing their love and support as we navigate our new course through life without them physically present. The curse is in our unwillingness to let the old relationship alter and change now that the dynamics are totally different, potentially holding us back from exploring the new life ahead of us. We want things to remain "the same," but, of course, they cannot.

I see this play out most markedly within the widow's journey, especially when the couple lived an entire lifetime together before one of them died, or if they were still so madly in love as to view each other as soulmates when one was suddenly ripped from the equation. Even with the words, *'til death do us part* proclaimed at the marriage ceremony, a surviving spouse tends to keep the couple status alive long after they've put their beloved into the ground by way of keeping a portrait of them in their bedroom, continuing to wear their wedding ring (often moving it from the ring finger to a chain around the neck), and celebrating their anniversary for years after their spouse dies.

Some will move on immediately while others feel guilty if they even consider taking another lover or spouse. In any case, I believe it is important to acknowledge the widow's journey as a sacred time, a time of becoming reacquainted with oneself, a time to reflect and review a life lived together, and eventually, when ready, a time to build a brand-new life, one of our own choosing.

Before I could truly move on, I had to go through a period of reflection. I needed to come to terms with what had happened and try to learn from everything I experienced during my ten-year relationship with Leo because I had come to understand trouble and hardship offer opportunities to overcome something within that needs work, and our romantic relationships present us with the best ways to accomplish this work.

My first foray into the world of dating after Leo's death proved to be such an occasion. It was rich with various clues I could follow to learn more about myself as a codependent spouse. It was like the whole experience was offered up to me in the form of a life-like movie I could "watch," taking note of my own behavior and tendencies to want to please others, putting my own needs and desires second. I saw through similarities (because that is how the Universe works—giving us the same set of circumstances in many different scenarios until we finally get it) my relationship with Leo playing out with this new friend. This gave me a chance to recognize and address my own enabling and self-deprecating behaviors before any lasting damage could be done. Simply by paying attention, I was finally able to learn how to live authentically, even when romance was introduced to the equation, and that was a powerful revelation.

People often ask me why we have to go through hardship or feel pain in order to grow. The answer is quite simple. We don't seek change when we are comfy and cozy. We like feeling settled and in familiar surroundings and circumstances. Only when we are made to feel uncomfortable in some way do we, out of necessity, seek any real change, and change is a prerequisite to growth.

Even so, typically we can only connect the dots and see how an uncomfortable experience led (sometimes forced) us to make a change that eventually brought something into our lives we could be grateful for with hindsight. Think back through your life. How many times have you thought, *Oh, I see it now! If I hadn't lost that job last year, I never would have found this one where I am appreciated more, paid much better, and have met a wonderful new friend!* In a case like this, is it really a stretch to think, *Thank goodness I got fired from that old job*? When you choose to view the world through this perspective, you begin to see hardship and painful experiences as opportunities to make changes that indeed help us grow.

When it comes to the pain and hardship your spouse's death leaves at your door, I doubt any of us would ever want to say or even think, "Thank goodness they died." The human tendency to feel guilt over such a selfish thought will override the impulse. But why can't we grieve their loss *and* feel grateful for everything the experience gifted us at the same time?

If my son's death introduced me to my spirituality and my daughter's death taught me to work with concepts like acceptance more fully and surrender, then Leo's death ushered in a whole new era for me, one where I would "walk the talk," so to speak. I learned to completely *trust* the process. The changes I went through were scary, but I stepped forward into them anyway, assured my Soul knew what it was doing and would guide me to a safe landing.

By relaxing into the experience and releasing my ego-self's need to see everything as black or white, my whole world suddenly became more colorful, my experiences more meaningful.

You can see this play out in the following dialogue with Leo as I use my broadened perception of the world and its peoples to work through the moment in time when I had to stop being Leo's wife and let another into my heart. The whole process came again with a duality that was very noticeable…a dread and sorrow over the *final ending* right in tandem with a charged excitement over the possibilities of finding new love.

If you've ever lost a spouse or lover, you probably can relate. The struggle is real as they say. We want a new life because we are still living and breathing, longing for love, but we feel torn and sometimes even guilty when we offer our hearts to another. But remember when I said our romantic relationships often present the most potent of life's lessons? Since I knew this to be true, I walked into the next chapter of my life with my eyes wide open, looking for those opportunities, and I was not disappointed.

Are you rooting for me? Excited that I am venturing out into the world, ready to let love back in? It certainly was a pivotal time in my life, the dawning of a new age so to speak…or so I thought. But instead of offering me a new and lasting love, my Soul had something else in mind. Let's take a look at the opportunities the Universe presented to me and how I responded to each one. I think you'll be surprised how things played out for me. I know I was!

(Dear Leo cont.)

I remember the day I truly stopped being your wife, Leo. Your death surely did not part us as archaic marriage vows would have one believe. No, I didn't stop being your wife until a couple of weeks before Christmas of 2014, two full years after you left, when our giant, all-natural Christmas tree came crashing down in the middle of the night.

You'll notice I used the word *our*, as if including you in the ritual of cutting a nine-foot tree to adorn our dining room each holiday season. Because up until that night, I still honored you and your presence in our lives and our home as my husband, my Leo. Absolutely I did.

A switch was thrown within me as I stood staring at that beast of a tree no longer reaching for the thousands of stars shining down on it through our oversized skylight, but instead, laying on the floor with its glass ornaments shattered and scattered like the dreams I once had of a life with you.

I cried softly to myself while dismantling that tree, reliving all the ways I thought I had been honoring your memory, but in reality, I was doing them to keep you alive and there with me on our property. Things like building a living memorial for you in what used to be your vegetable garden, a project that physically hurt me to maintain and kept me from other activities I would rather enjoy. And your lawn, Leo. I had been knocking myself out trying to keep your lawn as perfectly trimmed and fed as you did, but I could never quite achieve the beautiful carpet effect that seemed to come so easily to you.

But I did all those things willingly. I needed that process. It was a sacred time for me—for anyone who loses a life partner, I would think. I needed the time to gently come to an understanding like the one becoming clear that night while Sky and my sister slept in their rooms nearby. I realized it was time to let you go, to truly begin to live for myself, and not shape my world around keeping your memory as my husband alive. To do that, I had to stop thinking of you as my husband and let the relationship evolve into what it wanted to be going forward.

This saddened me, but it also excited me as I felt a charge of hope while I dragged that heavy tree outside all by myself and heaved it over the deck railing where it landed on the fresh, powdery snow-covered ground without a sound in the forest that was now my home and no longer ours.

I noticed the irony of the scene unfolding in how the lack of sound when that big, heavy tree hit the ground, marking a pivotal point in my grief journey, was much the same as the puny firecracker pop that heralded the moment you left this world. Just like that day, I had expected something louder and larger to mark such an occasion.

I felt you with me the next day when I went to Home Depot after work to buy a small, manageable, artificial Christmas tree. I heard you chuckle then just as clearly as I can hear it now while I write this in the company of flashing memories of manhandling that fallen tree in the middle of the night while still in my pajamas, instead of waking the others to help.

I felt you with me during the car ride home with my victorious purchase in the back, as if you knew what I had planned to do next, even before

I realized it myself and made sure you'd be there to help, support, and love me while I did.

You know how I cherished that voicemail, the one of you singing "You Are My Sunshine" but replacing sunshine with my name? I know you held me in your ethereal embrace more than once while I obsessively listened to it over and over in the early months of my widowhood.

And you knew I'd listen to it for the last time that day before deleting it once and for all as a means or ceremony of sorts to mark my intention to let go. Not let go of you, Leo, because I don't think I would ever want to do that, but letting go of you in the role of husband.

You began to show up in my life as more of a "guide" presence after that, getting my attention to warn me if I was neglecting something around the house or property, often signaling me in ways that would remind me to check the salt level in the water system right when it was about to run out or to put Drano in the bathroom sink before a clog formed, which was always inevitable with that particular drain.

As much as I appreciated those little Post-it notes to help keep the home front humming, I more fully enjoyed the way you guided me in life, like when I first decided it was time to open myself to the possibility of finding love again, almost three years after your death.

Since work, the house, and property, along with raising Skyla, took up most of my waking hours each day, I decided to give online dating a try. What did I have to lose? Perhaps I'd find a friend, a lover, or at the very least, learn to "put myself out there," as they say, a daunting task to be sure for those of us who've lost their life partner in such a painful and tragic way.

Before long, I felt a pull, an instinctive draw to a particular man I initiated contact with. We immediately began enjoying meaningful conversations on the phone. How lovely it was to have male energy in my world again!

In one of our earliest chats, we discovered a common thread that blew us both away—we simply could not chalk it up to coincidence. When the story of your suicide came out in conversation, he met me not with the silence of others who are shocked and at a loss for words, but with a tale of his own experience with a former girlfriend who had also taken her life in recent years.

This coincidence felt like it had your name written all over it, Leo. Once again, I was given a breadcrumb trail to follow down a path that would lead me on a journey of healing to my final destination of self-awareness, forgiveness, and heart-opening love.

He and I quickly became the very best of friends, and we enjoyed hours and hours of deep, meaningful, soul-searching conversations during those first few months while we became acquainted. Ours was one of the most authentic relationships I had ever experienced. We talked about anything and everything with honesty and complete abandon because we both sensed in each other a safe, judgment-free zone where we could be our true selves—no masks, no placating one another, no trying to change each other, and no strings attached.

Of course, I wondered if this friendship was leading to a deeper, more romantic union, so I decided to ask you in an intentional meditation if you thought this man was the one for me.

As it often did, your reply came quickly as a voice in my head. "Just be his friend, Vic…. Just be his friend." By then I had grown so fond of him I decided to convince myself you must be wrong. Surely, this growing love we had for one another was meant to be more than just platonic.

It didn't take long to notice things between us changed once we entered into a physical relationship. Sure, it was fun, but I noticed things about myself, my behavior, and my thoughts that caused me to wonder if I had made a mistake. I started holding back, no longer showing him my true self, the intimacy we shared as friends somehow dissolving when it should have been deepening. Soon, we both realized we worked much better as friends than as lovers, so yes, Leo, you were right. I should have just been a friend to him all along.

Even so, I cannot regret my actions because my ever-growing and expanding spiritual practice had taught me to believe there are many different paths we can choose, all leading to the golden kingdom of self-awareness and Soul-expansion. We are evolving as a species, and it is a much more interesting ride if we consciously engage in the process of our evolution than just being swept along by the tides of change.

I absolutely loved it when, still confused about what my relationship with this man I had so much love for was meant or not meant to become, I sought a reading with one of my favorite mediums, Stephanie.

You were always so quick to present yourself to her and speak frankly, offering just what I needed to hear at the time. Even she had to laugh when I told her I had gone against your advice to "just be his friend" and you immediately fired back with, "I'm glad you went against me because even though it didn't work out well, it was exactly what your Soul needed at the time."

That turned out to be true on so many levels. I went on to maintain a friendship with this man who often reminded me of a softer version of you, one without the complications of alcoholism. He had a similar temperament to yours, flying high on life one minute, then lashing out verbally when his feathers were ruffled the next. I was being presented with an opportunity to work through some of the codependent behavior I had developed living with you under the frequent assault of your mood-swings and fits of anger. So, in the end, yes, that relationship was a perfect fit for me at that time in my life.

I just love the way the Universe presents opportunities like this. My spirits are lifted every time a bizarre synchronicity or coincidence shows up. Honestly, the little thrill I get from making a connection to the unseen forces around me truly brings me the greatest joy.

I'm not talking about the joy we experience when we spend an evening laughing with friends or when we get an unexpected raise at work. No, I'm referring to a deeper experience, an all-inclusive one like the first time I drove the Slea Head Loop on the Dingle Peninsula in Ireland in search of *the new me,* and the scenic vistas took my breath away.

When the first expansive view of that famed coastline opened up, I was so overwhelmed by the raw and natural beauty of the place that I had to pull over, get out of my car, and just gape at the scene before me with my mouth hanging open. The experience flooded me with so much gratitude to be alive and be able to stand there bearing witness to such blinding natural beauty. I was filled with so much emotion that I didn't think my physical body could hold it all, so I cried. The tears of joy just flowed and flowed as assorted emotions, like gratitude, faith, love, appreciation, peace, acceptance, and a strong sense of connection to all flooded my entire being.

I remember that moment well because I had completely surrendered, body-mind-and-spirit, to the powerful sensations the view before me evoked. In that most precious moment, I realized the enormous gift that gush of tears was as it served me in so many more ways than just an expression of joy.

When my tears flowed uninhibited by shame, fear, frustration, anger, guilt, or pain, they opened the floodgates, giving any bottled-up feelings the freedom they craved to be expressed. I recognized the shift because it felt suddenly huge, heavy, and exhausting, although anyone watching would only have seen a woman crying silently as she looked out at this beautiful wonder of nature.

As the scene genuinely took my breath away, it also left my mind momentarily "off duty." My mind stuttered in its never-ending barrage of thoughts geared mostly toward judging my experience from moment to moment. Suddenly, I could clearly see how my mind had been playing guardian all my life. I had assigned my rational thought process the task of reigning over my life in all areas, guarding against any uncomfortable or unwanted experiences. I finally understood what all the spiritual teachers and gurus meant when they said, "the ego self" and how we must learn to disengage it or quiet it somehow to experience a deeper connection to the Soul-self.

Once the emotions were spent and I climbed back into my tiny little rental car, my ego-mind reengaged and immediately started to analyze what had just happened. As I replay this memory today, I can't help being reminded of another time, years before that experience, when my mind was also tricked into looking the other way so another layer of grief over my son's death could come up. I don't recall ever really thanking you for your part in that particular story, so I'd like to take a moment to do so now.

Leo, you were my rock in so many ways back then. You had so much patience and compassion for me when my pain was in the driver's seat. As helpless and inadequate as we all feel when we awkwardly try to "say the right thing" to a friend in deep grief, you always managed to come up with creative ways to hold me up when I stumbled, and I'll be forever grateful to you for that. I felt so blessed to have you at my side.

About two weeks after Adam's death, an innocent intention to lie next to me on the bed while I rested in the middle of the afternoon turned into a gentle expression of physical love. The longing for each other was still clearly alive and well, but the energy of it felt a bit fragile, as if the big G (Grief) was in the bed with us, ready to distract one or both of us at any moment, which, of course, would spoil the mood.

I had all the emotions one would expect as my self-talk tried to assert itself in the form of words like, "How could I possibly think about sex at a time like this?" and "It's only been two weeks—you don't really think you'll enjoy this do you?" and even, "What would other people think if they knew I was initiating sex when my teenaged son was barely cold in his grave? How could I possibly be so selfish?"

I could also tell, although we never talked much about it, you were having similar doubts. You were being uncharacteristically slow, easy, and gentle, always letting me take the lead to advance us to the next steps, never rushing me or assuming it was okay to proceed. Oh, how I loved you for that!

But want it I did, and at some point, that want became a need. I needed this intimate, lazy afternoon time with you. I needed to get out of my head for even just a few moments, and I needed the physical pleasure of sex. I needed to feel alive.

I remember your sweet expression of disbelief when I took things to the next level by encouraging you to take off your clothes while I did the same. And still, you just held me close, even though I knew it was driving you mad with your own desires and needs. Over those couple of weeks, you must have missed your lover and the closeness we had developed. I'm sure you wondered if things would ever be the same between us and how it would alter the woman you had fallen for. Would you still love me after all this?

But love me you did, and you did it very well that day, my Leo. You simply offered yourself to me to take what I wanted and needed, with no concern for your own pleasure or satisfaction. As I climbed on top of your beautiful male form and settled myself in the saddle, I became aware of how the grief had moved off and allowed me to feel something other than pain. I recall feeling extremely grateful that something in my life actually felt good, not quite what I'd call exciting or joyful, but we could certainly tiptoe around with feeling "good" for now.

Still, I assumed I would not be able to let enough of the all-consuming grief go to reach a climax, so when it did arrive, it took me completely by surprise. As the pleasure built in intensity, and my mind ceased to hold my attention, I was able to give myself over to that exquisite release.

Just as quickly and suddenly as it had arrived, the orgasm abruptly ended as something broke deep inside me. I collapsed forward, spilling hot tears onto your chest while my body heaved with gut-wrenching sobs instead of the lovely little after-shock spasms that normally follow sexual satisfaction.

I sensed then that you were at a loss. You didn't know what to say or do to help me. In that moment of confusion, you simply held me while the sorrow drained from me until I lay quietly, our bodies still entwined.

I know it killed you, Leo, as you always prided yourself on being able to swoop in and rescue those close to you when they were in distress. It made you feel good about yourself, like you had a grand purpose in life, but I can tell you now that just being present and allowing my grief to express itself in your company was exactly the thing I needed the most. So, thank you, Leo. Thank you for allowing me the space I needed to heal and for staying by my side throughout the journey.

Even with all that transpired over the years as you fought to control your alcoholism and your temper, my heart still explodes with love and compassion for you when I look back at that day. It was a poignant moment I will never forget because it was then I realized fun, joy, and peace could cruise right alongside grief, pain, and sorrow on this crazy ride we call life. Moments like those saved my sanity, and they encourage me to keep moving forward as I face life's biggest challenges.

That realization was probably one of the biggest gifts my grief over losing Adam brought, because it gave me the freedom to begin to dream of a new life while still living with the hurt and pain of the old one, and boy did that come in handy after you died, my Leo!

I find it poetically appropriate it was you who unknowingly led me to that precious discovery some ten years before your own suicide, which left me feeling completely shattered, alone, and abandoned while simultaneously sensing a new life of hope and freedom just up the road around the next corner.

Even though I could not see such a life, willingness to believe it was there waiting for me allowed me to move through the worst of the trauma and pain with a solid "knowing" that, once again, I would be okay. Not only would I be okay, but I would rebuild my life from the ground up, and this time, what I created would be for me, born of my desires, hopes, dreams, and wishes.

*"When the storm hits, I will reach out for you, as
the storm passes, I will build something new."*

(Excerpt from the song, "Surviving the Storm" by Vicky Edgerly)

What did rebuilding my life after widowhood look like? Nothing terribly special, really. It looked like a string of small, mundane tasks I didn't realize were huge on the difference-it-would-make-in-me scale, like cleaning out the woodstove to prepare to sell it when I stopped using it a year or so after my husband died, which derailed me emotionally when I realized I wouldn't be warmed by the wood Leo insisted on cutting himself to provide for his family ever again.

My new life also presented itself as big, end-of-an-era life events happening in bites so small you don't realize the change is taking place until it comes to completion, like the aging and eventual demise of the three dogs Leo and I raised from pups on our beautiful property in the woods. Losing the last of the "Ellis Boyz" was heart-breaking for me, and naturally, brought more bouts of fresh grief.

It looked like snapshots of vacations with the grandkids and lunches full of laughter with friends and quiet hours in the dark, contemplating the All-That-Is or finding fellowship in spiritual workshops and mystical excursions with groups of like-minded people. And it looked like sinks full of dirty dishes, weekly laundry to get through, a waxing and waning dedication to health and fitness, and a growing love for solo travel, born of a need to get to know my true self better and discover what I was made of.

But what of the grief during this time? What had become of it as the months marched into years? The following pages will give you a clear view into the eyes of grief from one who learned to look instead of shying away. Watch next as my relationship with grief deepens and my understanding of it expands, settling me into the luxurious state of peace I predominantly reside in now, knowing you too can have a similar experience if you choose to reach for it. And I sincerely hope you reach for it. What do you have to lose?

"There is a sacredness in tears.
They are not the mark of weakness, but of power.
They speak more eloquently than ten thousand tongues.
They are the messengers of overwhelming grief,
of deep contrition, and of unspeakable love."

— *Washington Irving*

CHAPTER 14

GRIEF, A LASTING RELATIONSHIP

During my first grief journey, I recognized my pain was something of an enigma. I didn't want to be in pain anymore. I appreciated those close to me who could sit with me and my pain, those who didn't turn away when I dropped my veil and exposed the true nature of it, the ugliness that it was. I appreciated those Souls who could do that, the ones who could do that silently without agendas of their own—the ones who didn't try to take my pain away from me. It was *mine*. It was mine alone, and no one could take it. I would learn to resent those who tried. So, yes, I guarded my pain like a jealous lover.

Today, I still sit alone with my grief, but it looks a lot different now. Like lovers in a longtime relationship, we have both changed a lot along the way. It's quieter now. We know each other so well after all these years that we can sit with each other in silence. We can just *be* together in the same room without one spoken word. I no longer need to name it. I know what it wants from me when it shows up. I no longer need to search for reasons, to demand answers. I know what it wants, and I surrender. I yield to its needs, and I walk willingly into the familiar embrace. I allow the pain, dulled by years of experience, tamed by my own stubborn struggle to "not let it win," to envelope my whole being. I rest my head on its shoulder as we embrace, and I allow the full richness of the penetrating sorrow to enter my being. I *allow* it—I understand its needs.

I used to think grief came to consume me. Like an invasive cancerous thing that we, by nature, are designed to hate, to fight against at all cost. I used to think that, before I got to know it by name: *Grief.*

Turns out I misunderstood what it wanted. It doesn't want to fight. To do so only creates more struggle, like thrashing about while trying to escape barbed wire. I'd only become more entangled and suffer more harm from the many barbs in the long run, for this is a battle that can't be won.

No, surrendering in trust is really the best way through from what I've learned along the way.

It doesn't want to be pushed down, ignored, or conquered. To do so only traps it in the physical body where it will take up residence and breed among my tissue and organs, eventually showing up on an MRI as a disease, injury, or tumor.

So, what does it want? I thought it wanted to be *transformed*—changed, altered, and shaped by me into something beautiful and wonderful, something I could bring to the world and say, "Look! See? Grief doesn't have to be so painful. It doesn't have to destroy us. We can *transform* it into a beautiful musical ballad or mesmerizing piece of artwork for all to love and admire. Grief doesn't have to be scary!"

But even as noble as that endeavor sounds, it is not at all what grief really wants. Only after I passed through all the bargaining, the fighting, the "work" of transforming it did I finally give in to it and let it pass *through* me. That is when the light finally came on.

My grief just wants to know I understand it, that I see it for what it is—an *energy*. A big energy. One that won't be denied, destroyed, or even transformed. What it wants is to be *felt, seen,* and *acknowledged.* Once it has what it wants, it leaves all on its own, returning less and less frequently as the years go by, but now, when I answer the knock and see it standing on the threshold, instead of slamming the door in its face, I invite it in and pull it into a warm embrace. My long-lost friend, whom I know so well, who knows *me* so well, has come for a visit. Come sit for a while. You are welcome in my home.

And in exchange for my hospitality, grief does something for me each time it visits. It removes another layer of pain and suffering and takes it with them when it goes, leaving me lighter, wiser, and more capable of handling any perceived struggle that comes my way.

So, yes, my grief is mine. It's the most intimate relationship in my life. We've been together for so long now I can sometimes intuit when it will visit next and occasionally miss it when it's gone. I think of it fondly and reminisce about days when we didn't get along so well. I rejoice in how far we have come.

Grief is the one relationship we can never leave, throw out, divorce, or ignore.

Scores of people may tell you, "You will never get over your grief." The more positive thinkers will go on to say, "While you'll never get over the death of your loved one, you can learn to live with it," and I suppose I must admit there is some truth in those statements. But as you can tell by my own natural tendency to put a positive spin on things, I immediately want to reframe them into statements that leave me feeling more hop*eful* and less hop*eless.*

"You will never get over your grief," becomes, "Grief is a natural part of life and is now woven into my story, but it does not define who I am or how I live." And, "You can learn to live with it" becomes "No one can live through what I have and come out unchanged, but I know I am in charge of who I become. I can choose to learn and grow from this experience."

Can you *feel* the difference between the original statements and the reframed versions? Maybe we do carry aspects of our grief with us forever, and that's okay as long as we see it for what it is, part of our life story, and we no longer fear it. In this way, it becomes part of the whole picture that is our life, indiscernible by the naked eye, and only revealed to new friends during naturally evolving conversations.

The grief itself will change and fade in its stature and significance if you let it. The choice to move beyond the symptoms of grief (like deep sorrow, high-anxiety, uncontrollable emotions, anger, or depression) really is yours and yours alone. But once made, the Universe will move heaven and earth to make it attainable for you. Every step of the way you will encounter the choice to continue on your mission to learn and grow or stop at any time if you become comfortable with the status quo.

Take this book for instance. You somehow became aware of it. Perhaps it was recommended by a friend or maybe an advertisement just popped up in your news feed. Some would believe having a book like this show up just when they need it is Divine Intervention—a God wink extraordinaire. But here's the thing, you could have chosen not to read it. I, for one, am glad you did read it!

WITH A LIVING EXAMPLE, YOU BEGIN TO BELIEVE

Well, here we are, you and I bound together in this memorable moment in time. You, bearing witness to a story that could have belonged to either of us, but in the end, was allotted specifically to me and my family.

You watched as I picked myself up and stumbled forward, lost and broken, blindly searching for a healing path that didn't seem to exist after my son Adam took his own life at the tender age of eighteen.

You saw hope and understanding bloom within me as that first dance with grief led me to the mystical world of *Spirit* and *Faith* where I was introduced to life-altering concepts like realizing I have a choice in how I feel and react to circumstances, proving that changing my perspective can change my experience.

You received evidence that encountering my son in his bodyless form through lucid dreams and earthly signs and synchronicities helped ease me into acceptance and opened my mind to working with other metaphysical and/or conscious-living concepts and modalities like reiki healing,

Shamanic journeying, and rooting out old beliefs (rewiring my brain by training it to believe a different, more empowering story).

You watched me carry those precious seeds of knowledge, holding them close as I unknowingly headed straight into the two-year task of walking my daughter to her own early grave next to her brother. You traveled with me as I brought forth what I had learned about the nature of the Soul and our plotted destinies, effectively easing my own suffering through an extremely challenging time as I relaxed more fully into the process of surrender that her cancer demanded of me.

Perhaps you were as surprised as I was when my shadow-self showed up and claimed her place among the generations of women in our family, an unexpected side effect of doing purposeful grief-work that I consider a great treasure. The irony of the similarities between this aspect of myself and my husband Leo's bullying behavior was not lost on either of us, I'm sure. (This one little unexpected gift helped me understand, empathize, and forgive my husband's transgressions on much deeper levels after all these years, leaving me feeling peaceful and without regret after all I endured during that relationship.)

You felt the suspense and foreboding of Leo's approaching suicide as you crowded into the car with me and my uninvited passenger, the Grim Reaper, that momentous summer day. Perhaps you watched in disbelief as the scene played out in your mind's eye of his newly widowed wife kneeling on the bloodied forest floor in the midst of her shock and turmoil to offer reiki healing to her beloved's Soul.

And finally, you breathed a sigh of relief to learn yet another traumatic death scene did not undo me, but instead, served to help me grow spiritually and claim a wonderful new life of my choosing, all while teaching me how to truly love and accept myself along the way.

Were you stunned to realize how valuable walking consciously through a grief journey can be as it teaches us everything we need to know about how to live a more meaningful and fulfilling life?

Did you cheer for me then? When I stood tall after all I had endured, did you rejoice in how steadfastly I persevered through back-to-back, life-altering events? And did it surprise you to feel that way toward a woman who has suffered such "tragedy"?

I'm asking you these questions because simply noticing your mind's ability to shift between seeing an event as "good or bad," "tragedy or opportunity" will go a long way in your efforts to retrain your mind to think more empowering thoughts, should you decide to give it a try, and it's always easier for us to see the truth of this playing out in someone else's life than our own, so this is a great place to start.

If you're anything like me, once you see a living example, you begin to believe. You feel that tiny spark of hope whispering in your ear, hinting there is another way—a better way.

But is grief actually curable? Have you been anxiously awaiting the final punchline, the part of my story where I tell you my grief is gone? Cured? Never to be seen or

If you're anything like me, once you see a living example, you begin to believe. You feel that tiny spark of hope whispering in your ear, hinting there is another way—a better way.

heard from again? Well, that part will never be written. Not by me anyway. And do you know why? It's simple really.

Grief is not an illness or disease, so there is no need for a cure. It's merely an energy that storms into one's life after a perceived loss, and as an energy, it cannot be destroyed, corralled, or banished. It really just needs to be understood and acknowledged, not treated like an illness and stuffed down with pills, denial, or distractions.

If we, as a society, can reach further into understanding it, we can begin to see that this big energy is of our own making. Humanity has chosen it as our collective and common reaction when someone we love dearly leaves the fold. We summon this huge ball of pain, equal in measure to, but the polar opposite of, the force of love we feel for the person who has left our physical world. We all know this at a very primal level. And since it can be said that the opposite of *love* is *fear*, this explanation makes perfect sense. We have been taught that grief is an expression of love…but it's actually an expression of fear.

We fear we cannot live without the deceased, and we fear we won't survive the pain. We fear we are losing our sanity, and many fear for their financial stability if they've lost a contributing partner in the household. We fear for our futures, how they will unfold, and how we will manage the fast-moving changes in our lives when someone close to us dies. We are afraid of navigating a new and strange world without our loved one, and we fear what we will become, having gone through such a life-altering event. We are afraid to say "goodbye," the finality of it, and indeed, we fear the inevitability of our own eventual death.

Once we understand something a little better, we no longer fear it, and once we remove the fear, we have less and less anxiety, panic, heartache, depression, and sorrow, leaving room for things like calm, peace, contentment, spiritual connection, and yes, even joy to come back into our lives.

So, how will you choose to walk through your next grief experience? After reading this book, will you be more apt to have faith in your innate capabilities to cope, or will you become fixated on the archaic and depressing things society would have us believe about the grief journey, things that leave us feeling we'll never experience joy again?

And what of your children, grandchildren, nieces, and nephews? Will you speak openly about death as a natural part of life, teaching them grief is an expected guest after someone we love leaves the earth, or will you, like many others, continue to "shield" them from such a disturbing subject, leaving them to flounder, searching for relief from the pain that will inevitably show up on their doorstep like I had to do after my son died?

I hope, of course, you will gain enough fuel from this story to power you through when you come face to face with my old friend, Grief. My heartfelt wish is for you to carry a seed of hope within your heart so when that crusty old bastard comes knocking on your door, you can say, "I know who you are, and I am not afraid."

And while you may not be able to let Grief in at first, simply looking it straight in the face for starters will immediately place you among the ranks of survivors because in doing that, you have made a conscious choice *not* to live as a victim.

Once we don our survival hat, some of us experience a burning desire or passion for helping others suffering from similar circumstances. We get so excited over our discoveries—even the smallest adjustments in our way of thinking can create *big* results in how we feel about our situation— we simply must share with others. Our hearts crack open and we want to give back. Somewhere deep inside, we understand we are all connected, and when we help lift another toward healing, we also accelerate our own efforts to overcome.

Perhaps this is you. Perhaps being exposed to a story like mine is all you need to propel you along your healing path. But if you feel you need more support, I hope you can love yourself enough to reach out for that help. Find a reputable therapist with experience helping folks process acute grief. Take a yoga class specifically designed to release grief from the body. Use empowering tools developed by others who have walked this path before you like the ones I offer in *Dragonfly Wisdom: A Holistic Approach to Grief Support* or book a private session with a grief journey guide like myself, who has a proven record of inspiring others to grow from their devastating loss.

At sixty, I find I am no longer grieving the loss of my husband or children, for those emotions played themselves out long ago. No, there are no more tears of pain. Now when a memory catches me by surprise, the tears that flow are tears of *love*, how grief should truly look. I feel no panic, denial, or sorrow. They have been replaced with peace, acceptance, and hope. The tears I cry now are the tears of a heart bursting with love and joy, similar to what one experiences watching a particularly romantic or uplifting scene in a movie.

My life here on the Gulf Coast of Florida is abundant in all ways that are important to me. I live in this paradise-like environment with a never-ending sense of adventure to explore. I enjoy bountiful experiences in nature since I am surrounded by top-notch beaches, where I can walk for miles, and beautifully groomed hiking trails and botanical gardens that offer a feast for the eyes and other senses. There is fellowship here at any number of local churches and spiritual gatherings when I choose to engage, and I have the love and support of close friends and a handful of family members who have also relocated to this area. Yes, my life is rich and full.

When I look in the mirror today, I sometimes wonder if my smile is genuine. Is it a real smile or one I learned to paste on my face somewhere along the way? But then my gaze falls on my eyes, and I see the truth of it all. In the sparkle, I see the mischievous child. I see all the joys life has brought me in these eyes. I see the stunning beauty of the world and its people, and in the dark, liquid depths, where one might expect to find hidden sorrow, I see the wisdom of the ages.

The End
(*Or is this just the beginning?*)

"If home is where the heart is, and mine is open wide,
then sadness, pain, and sorrow…they have no place to hide.
For all you weary travelers who've come from far and wide,
with my heart truly open now, I'll welcome you inside."

(Excerpt from the song, "Home" by Vicky Edgerly)

ABOUT THE SONGS

The lyrics sprinkled throughout this book come from songs I wrote about my journey through the grief storm. Processing grief and/or expressing pain can be done quite nicely through creative expression. Using the creative side of your brain to make a tangible piece of art while in the middle of a difficult life challenge is a great way to calm the mind and soothe the Spirit. This is why teaching emotional release through a creative path is used quite heavily within the DFW method for supporting the grief journey.

While it was never my intention to perform my songs in public or market them in any way, I did have the pleasure of working with some professional musicians I knew at the time who set them to music and created high-quality studio recordings of them for me.

Since I had never sung a note in my life other than the occasional sing-along in a bar in my youth, stepping into the recording studio for the first time offered an opportunity to practice facing my fear of "being seen," a fear I volunteered to overcome because I would need public speaking skills to bring my message of hope and healing after great loss to a larger audience than those I encountered in my private practice as a grief journey guide.

So, the songs, while professionally recorded, are not what I would call "market ready" in any way. It's just me and my untrained vocals giving voice to my journey through grief, pain, and eventual emergence into the light of understanding and a healed self. If you are curious and wish to hear them,

I've published them on my YouTube channel so my descendants will have access to them long after I leave this world.

You can find them at the following URLs:

"Surviving the Storm" by Vicky Edgerly

https://www.youtube.com/watch?v=Sys-bWCHmJs

"Home" by Vicky Edgerly

https://www.youtube.com/watch?v=85x7opAtkdI

"Did You See Me?" by Vicky Edgerly

https://www.youtube.com/watch?v=MrOazzjGOi4

"Deep grief sometimes is almost like a specific location, a coordinate on a map of time. When you are standing in that forest of sorrow, you cannot imagine that you could ever find your way to a better place. But if someone can assure you that they themselves have stood in that same place, and now have moved on, sometimes this will bring hope."

— Elizabeth Gilbert

ABOUT THE AUTHOR

Vicky Edgerly uses the wisdom she's gained through study and personal experience to assist others in navigating life's challenges. As someone who has chosen to grow from her STEs (Spiritually Transformative Events), she uses her knowledge and experience to empower others. She specializes in showing folks the way through the grieving experience by applying a holistic approach (addressing the body-mind-spirit connection) and offers private sessions as a "Grief Journey Guide." She has worked closely with The Afterlife Education Foundation from Portland, Oregon, for several years and was featured in open panel discussions at their annual conferences. She is the author of a popular blog called "Let's Talk About the Elephant in the Room—Frank Discussion About Difficult Things" and developed an innovative grief support system called, *Dragonfly Wisdom: A Holistic Approach to Grief Support*. She currently lives in St. Petersburg, Florida, where she looks forward to retirement, which she plans to spend traveling and educating others about the taboo subject of grief.

You can learn more about Vicky and the services she offers by visiting her website at:

www.WhiteElephantWisdom.com

- Vicky's blog can be found at: www.whiteelephantwisdom.blogspot.com
- Find Vicky's photography store at: https://vicky-edgerly.pixels.com/

Connect with Vicky on social media:

- https://www.facebook.com/whiteelephantwisdom/
- https://www.youtube.com/@whiteelephantwisdomwithvic5720

Contact Vicky at:

VickyAfterLife@gmail.com

info@WhiteElephantWisdom.com

DRAGONFLY WISDOM

- A Holistic Approach to Grief Support -

What Is Dragonfly Wisdom?

Dragonfly Wisdom is an innovative system designed to help guide those actively grieving through the painful journey of loss in a constructive and empowering way. The book is formatted as a step-by-step instruction manual for individuals and groups interested in facilitating much-needed community grief support groups and implements a holistic healing approach with a focus on *self-healing* and *soul growth*, typically resulting in a gentler and more meaningful grieving experience for participants.

Where did it come from?

Vicky Edgerly developed this comprehensive program after spending a decade studying the effects acute and/or prolonged grief can have on individuals or families. Her passion for this work surfaced after her eighteen-year-old son Adam took his own life on Mother's Day in 2002. When she sought solace within a local grief support group, she discovered a "blind-leading-the-blind" process that left her feeling hopeless. She believed there was a better way, and she vowed to find it.

Edgerly went on to experience two more traumatic losses when her thirty-year-old daughter Tierra succumbed to cancer in 2010, followed by her husband Leo's dramatic suicide in 2012. These experiences where put to good use because Vicky was able to bring her growing knowledge into those successive grief journeys and test her theories on herself before compiling her wisdom (knowledge gained through personal experience) into this gentle, yet powerful system for traversing the grief journey.

What makes this system innovative?

The Dragonfly Wisdom method helps folks no matter where they are on their grief journey in ways that leave attendees feeling supported and less fearful about what they are going through. This support can significantly ease the severe anxiety often associated with the grief journey. Unlike traditional support groups where all attendees are gathered together, the DFW program separates the healing journey into *two distinct phases.*

Why two phases?

Edgerly recognized early on that placing folks experiencing acute grief in the same room with folks who are consciously engaged in using the grief experience as an invitation to grow and expand, both personally and spiritually, is not a productive way to facilitate effective self-healing.

When someone in extreme pain encounters others who seem to be past the early stages of grief, they can be inspired to survive, yes, but they may also feel intimidated and even ashamed of their own emotional reactions. This experience can result in a new habit of stuffing or hiding their true feelings.

Likewise, bringing the newly bereaved into a group that engages in lively discussions about ethereal messages they believe they've received from their deceased loved ones or actively celebrating the day they died as their "Spirit Birthday" can limit the group's freedom to fully explore the riches and "gifts" a life-altering experience like significant loss can bring. The group naturally feels *self-conscious* and a little *guilty* about flaunting their ability to experience joy in the face of their grief when in the presence of those in profound pain.

Think of it like triage when your body has suffered life-threatening injuries and you seek emergency treatment at your local hospital. First, you are assessed (intake interview) before going to the ICU (Phase One of DFW) where you receive critical care—staunching the "blood flow" (calming the fear and cooling the nervous system).

Next, you attend Physical Therapy (Phase Two of the DFW system), where it still "hurts" to do the work, but you are strong enough and ready to engage in a deeper healing experience and exploration of the *Self* with the intention of learning and growing from your painful experience.

How does it work?

Three basic principles are employed throughout this method:

1. Decide to survive. (We *do* have a choice.)

2. Attend to one sore spot at a time. (Focus on where you are *now*; don't look back or ahead.)

3. Dig up bones. (Replace old and damaging beliefs with more empowering ones.)

Phase One, also known as the "Story Tending Phase," focuses on supporting the newly bereaved or those who cannot move past the acute stages of grief by creating a safe, sacred space to share and explore their story of loss. This is a judgment-free environment where the pain of grief can be expressed freely and openly without shame. Our main goal here is to establish a supportive community environment and introduce exercises designed to lessen anxiety and calm the nervous system like mudras (a symbolic or ritualistic hand position used to open energy flow within the body-mind-spirit), breathing techniques, or even certain physical exercises and yoga poses.

Through helpful flow-charts, facilitators who have been coached to listen for and identify common beliefs that hold a person trapped in a repeating pain pattern can begin to introduce thought-provoking questions that gently guide attendees to discover new ways to think about their experience. Understanding they do, indeed, have a choice in how they perceive what has happened will gently guide them into acceptance where they begin to feel hopeful healing is possible.

With the facilitators' help, the bereaved decide to move into a **Phase Two** group when they feel ready to engage in group discussions without encountering severe emotional responses. The goals for Phase Two are to build on the community ties created in Phase One, consciously work on identifying and rooting out old beliefs that are keeping folks attached to their pain, and introduce candid discussions of death and the possibility of an afterlife.

Meetings in Phase Two groups use a variety of methods to keep folks consciously aware of how their grief story is playing out in their lives and what their role is in how they are feeling about the process. The DFW manual offers examples of thought-provoking questions to lead empowering discussions and heart-opening activities like altar building or creating ritual and ceremony that introduce a sense of honor and sacredness to the grief journey.

Additionally, guided meditations using "suggestive imagery" serve to gently train the mind to look at things from different angles. Change your perception and your whole life changes!

What if I don't feel comfortable in a Phase Two group?

The Dragonfly Wisdom method is designed to work with folks from all walks of life, all cultures, and all religious beliefs, no matter where they are in their grief journey. While Phase Two gives folks who wish to *grow from grief* a wonderful opportunity to work on rebuilding themselves within the comfort and security of the group setting, something no other community grief support program offers, others may simply want help getting past the worst of it, so Phase One is perfect for them.

Since grief is a very personal experience, facilitators of the DFW program are taught to take their cues from each bereaved individual. When their curiosity begins to override their pain, they are welcome to attend a Phase Two meeting. Likewise, if at any time things become too difficult or intense, they are welcome to move back into Phase One meetings for as long as needed.

What can I expect to get out of the program?

DFW is designed to be an expansive program where attendees choose their own level of participation. For some, it's enough to attend a Phase One group, a judgment-free zone where they can freely express their feelings and learn how to survive the intense grief by quelling some of the fear associated with sudden, significant loss. They're grateful for the support of others in similar circumstances who serve as living examples that survival is possible.

Others will continue on to Phase Two, which is designed to help folks change how they experience their grief by shifting it from a heavy burden to more of a sacred honor. They enjoy even deeper connections with their fellow bereaved, and many go on to engage in actively assisting others by volunteering or even running grief support groups themselves.

In either case, the goal is never to *eliminate* the sorrow associated with grief but simply to shift how it is experienced, which lessens the severity of symptoms like fear and anxiety. In this way, the bereaved remains in charge of their own healing path at all times.

**"We cannot transform the grief, but if we
are curious enough to open our hearts to the
experience, we can let the grief transform us."**

Please visit www.Dragonfly-Wisdom.com
to learn more and acquire your copy of the
Dragonfly Wisdom manual today!

NOTES:

NOTES:

NOTES:

NOTES:

www.ingramcontent.com/pod-product-compliance
Lightning Source LLC
Chambersburg PA
CBHW071453140726
47997CB00005B/1704

9 798999 338310